Dedication

This book is dedicated to all the Generation Y-er's, for their creative talents towards technology and innovation. Their natural actions and ability have reinforced in me the ingredients that are essential to master innovation.

To me, they are my heroes—always. I have always admired their personal qualities of curiosity, flexibility and intrigue.

For Generation Y-er's, their everyday life is filled with discovery, exploration, challenge and mastery. These are all positive characteristics that will hold them in good stead for the future.

Our future leaders will begin to emerge from a place where their world has no boundaries and technological advancements are tools to be used for activity, entertainment and day-to-day communications.

For they are tomorrow's heroes.

Today's leaders will benefit from learning to manage effectively the future generation's strengths and intellect in order to capture, ignite and unleash the generation's latent abilities.

As workplace leaders, this may well be our greatest challenge in the future. Our greatest conflict will be with ourselves and not with others.

Maybe the secrets of success lie with them and not us. It could well be that our role as leaders is to simply ask them where they see the future—as I often do. Because they automatically know that innovation comes from the fringes.

Greg Kinnaird

Greg Kinnaird is the Manager of Corporate Learning Solutions which was founded in 2000 to educate high potential leaders and teams to champion change and innovation. Greg holds a Master's in Business Administration and a Degree in Training and Development.

He has over 20 years of experience in Organisational Development, Talent Management and Learning / Leadership Development, specialising in the areas of developing high potential leaders to effectively manage teams and tasks.

Contents

Acknowledgements

I would like to acknowledge the many wonderful people who have supported me on this journey.

Firstly, past employers, employees and colleagues who have provided me with an environment of constant learning and development to be at my innovative best.

The 10,000 managers and leaders who have shared their insights throughout my leadership and team programmes that focus on developing champions of innovation.

To my parents and family networks who have provided me with an environment that stimulated thought and creativity, and allowed me to be the person I am today.

They may not know it but they have all shared this journey with me in mind and spirit.

∵ Preface

> *Achieving good performance is a journey, not a destination.*
>
> **Kenneth H Blanchard**
>
> *Author, speaker, business consultant*

Corporate Utopia – Finding Nirvana with High Potential Leaders is a compilation of stories and anecdotes from over 10,000 people I have worked with over the past 10 years. Without a doubt, they are the heroes of the day.

Throughout this book, you will gain unique insights into proven strategies that you can use immediately to harness the energy of your workplace.

I urge you to uncover the hidden gems, secrets, philosophies and inspirations that are offered to you throughout this book. You may also find the personal formulae for success that you have been searching for.

If you are looking to push the boundaries of innovation within your workplace, you will find the solution in this book. With an open mind, the solution could be found in the first sentence of the first paragraph of the first chapter. Look closely and you will find it. The solution will jump out from the page with a blinding flash of the obvious.

Remember that the quality of your thinking will determine the quality of your future. You will be amazed at the insights into what motivates people. You will discover what stifles innovation within your workplace on a day- to-day basis.

This book assumes that you are a professional individual who is dedicated to maintaining your competitive and innovative edge in the workplace and in your career. The intention of this book is to give you and your employees an easy road map that will allow you to openly discuss and challenge the innovation paradigms that currently exist in your workplace.

To become innovative requires breaking paradigms, challenging existing thinking and frameworks, and setting new boundaries.

I encourage you to check and challenge your current work processes so that you can add value, improve, prosper and profit.

It is important to note that this book is not about management theories and concepts. The findings and feedback found in this book are gleaned from thousands of managers and leaders who have told me what works and what does not work.

These heroes have contributed by sharing with me their

successes and challenges. They have also identified the key to being innovative for any organisation—the organisation must develop its leaders and teams to champion innovation.

Managers and leaders around the world have been eagerly awaiting the information contained in this book.

With an open mind, the secrets that are contained in this book will allow you to unlock the shackles so that you can master innovation today.

I personally look forward to meeting with you so that we can discuss your thoughts and ideas on mastering innovation. I would be interested to hear about your successes and challenges as you go in search of innovation.

Until then...enjoy all innovative things.

Greg Kinnaird

Manager and Author

(Organisational Development / Learning and Development / Talent Management)

⠼Introduction

Innovation is the specific instrument of entrepreneurship. The act that endows resources with a new capacity to create wealth.

Peter F Drucker

Pre-eminent management consultant

The Causes of Innovation Death

Innovation almost always dies a natural death within your workplace. By 'natural', I mean that its death is a normal part of a progression of events that occur in your organisation's life cycle. This is not necessarily the inevitable outcome, but it is by far the most common. Three factors usually conspire to kill innovation on the part of the individuals in your work team:

- Expansion
- Achievement
- Effectiveness

I'm sure you will agree that these are three very positive-sounding

11

words and they traditionally have great value in the conceptual system of management. Yet, the processes they represent are sooner or later the cause of the rigidity, fossilisation and lack of responsiveness that is so characteristic of your organisation.

Have you ever noticed how growth tends to kill innovation, simply because the elephant cannot move as quickly as the rabbit! There are several specific changes that will typically take place as your organisation gets larger and leaner. See if you can relate to any of the following:

Freeze: It takes longer for you to get anything accomplished because more people are involved. Remember that innovation requires results, not just ideas.

No-go power: As your organisation gets larger and leaner, you will have to get more organised. This means that more of your people develop what is known as 'no-go' power, and fewer have real 'go' power.

This type of culture will also start to impose sanctions on the mavericks within your work team.

Wipe out: You may find that two or more departments or workgroups may be competing with one another trying to gain more influential roles. There will be less sharing of ideas, less support for innovative approaches and more preoccupation with who is right and who is wrong within your workplace.

Lost leadership: As your organisation grows and downsizes due to market influences, you will discover that it becomes more difficult for the CEO to give personal and intellectual leadership to you and your team.

In a perverse way, the more successful your company is with a particular product, service or line of business, the higher the risk you run of neglecting other possibilities and opportunities. You may also find that success tastes so good that it will begin to dull the appetite for risk. Your people will spend their days, weeks, months and years trying to do things correctly in order to maximise operational performance.

Remember that your quest for perfection and quality will often stifle the process of innovation.

The Killer Phrases

I have a confession to make. I have attended a number of your workplace meetings and have created a list of seven of the all-time best 'Killer Phrases' that I have heard your team communicate verbally.

- A good idea but...
- All right in theory but...
- Be practical...
- Costs too much...
- It is not budgeted for...
- We have been doing it this way for a long time and it works...
- Too hard to implement...

Keep in mind that when you hear your team saying any of these 'Killer Phrases', you are actually hearing judgement or evaluation. Remind them that in the process of innovation, judgement comes after actively seeking alternatives, ideas or options.

How to Stimulate Innovative Thinking

There are various strategies you can use to stimulate innovation within your work team.

These strategies include approaches you can utilise with both internal and external sources.

Consider how easy it is for you to start the following actions today with very little effort, energy and cost:

- Put together focus groups that are made up of your internal and external customers.

- Provide the relevant infrastructure and resources to your team such as flip charts, a table covered in paper used for doodling and note-taking or even an electronic whiteboard.

- Be as concrete as you possibly can when coming up with innovative initiatives. Give your team direction and focus.

- Don't assume that this problem or challenge is similar to the ones that you and your team have previously come across.

- Stretch workplace goals for what you want to achieve and remember to set high aspirations for your people.

- Generate as many ideas as you can before you evaluate and prioritise them. Remember to suspend judgement until the creative ideas are tabled.

- Use a skilled facilitator to best utilise your team's time.

- Bring in paid or unpaid 'human resources' such as students and people seeking job transitions to break paradigms and old patterns of thinking and behaviour.

- Bring in a visitor from outside your workplace to participate in your creative thinking session.

- Bring back one of your former (now-retired) employees.

- Arrange reciprocal visits with organisations in other industries to stimulate and reinforce outside-the-box thinking for your team.

- Bring in a speaker from outside to present a unique perspective or expertise at your next creative meeting.

:ᐧ Corporate Utopia

– Finding Nirvana with High Potential Leaders

> *Good thoughts are no better than good dreams,*
> *unless they are executed.*
>
> **Ralph Waldo Emerson**

You are about to read a fable of four characters who embarked on a quest to engineer innovation in the work environment.

When you read this fable, think about your workplace and consider who best emulates the attributes of our four fictional friends: Dominus, Associus, Steadius and Perfectionus.

To get the best out of this book, you will need to get involved. Be prepared to examine your existing paradigms so that you can begin to understand what it takes to master innovation.

You may find this book interesting but challenging. You may also find it insightful but confronting. So if you are mentally ready, the journey to the magic land of Corporate Utopia is about to begin.

This book has been written using masculine forms for ease and simplicity. Switch the characters to the feminine as you read—if you wish. We encourage and suggest that you challenge and exercise your existing 'analytical' paradigms by replacing the four fictional characters with the names of 'real-life' people you work with.

By doing so, you will find that the characters spring to life whilst you are stretching the creative hemisphere on the right side of your brain. Try it. After all, regular exercise of the brain muscle is healthy.

As you read, remember to look for the hidden gems, secrets, philosophies and inspirations that are offered to you throughout the book. With an open mind, you will find immediate solutions that will hit you in the face when you least expect it.

See if you can spot your workplace employees that this fable has been based upon - Let the quest begin.

⁑The Challenge
- Ego and Performance

> *Innovation is not the product of logical thought,*
> *although the result is tied to logical structure.*
>
> **Albert Einstein**

Dominus, Associus, Steadius and Perfectionus had a dream of learning to effectively understand the way one another worked and thought. Together, they decided to embark on a quest in search of the magic land known as Corporate Utopia —a legendary place where they would learn all they needed to know about mastering innovation.

"Hooray!" they shouted in one voice as they enthusiastically started on their journey.

Dominus thought to himself: *I have a natural fear of failure, of losing control and of being manipulated. Therefore, I had better do this myself before anyone else does. Besides, who else could do the job as fast and as well as me?*

He stated his position instantly. "Follow me, because I have the loudest voice and I'm confident in directing and shaping you, and because I value quick results, challenge, control, power, ego, status and authority.

"I am sure that you too value the same as I," continued Dominus as he tried to marshall the group together.

Steadius and Perfectionus shook their heads in silent defiance. Surely, people will respect my loud voice and naturally follow me, mused Dominus.

At the same time however, Associus was feeling a little anxious and uneasy because he also had a brilliant idea about how to go in search of the magic land of Corporate Utopia. But he was scared of Dominus' loud and stern voice. He recalled that when he was a child, a stern and raised voice meant trouble. The memory caused Associus to revert to his old ways as he had always done as a child.

Interestingly, Associus continued to do this as a mature adult when the smell of potential conflict is in the air.

Unlike Dominus, Associus was a team player and valued harmony, being liked and accepted, and being recognised positively by his peers. Because of this, Associus often found that he said "yes" when he really meant "no" and this troubled him.

Many a restless night was spent tossing and turning on things that he had said "yes" to, when he should have stood his ground to clearly and confidently say "no".

Why do I let people talk me into things that I don't want to do? reflected Associus.

"Well, are you in or out, Associus? Hurry up and make a decision," barked Dominus.

"Yes," replied Associus reluctantly. *Yet another sleepless night of I-should-have, I-could-have, if-only-I-had-asserted-myself,* Associus thought to himself. He looked down at his trusty four-legged companion. Stroking its fur coat, Associus felt resentful because his fear of rejection and isolation had crippled his full potential to be his natural self.

His heart felt heavy and his eyes swelled with tears as he seemed to connect with the only living creature that did not prejudge him.

"Dominus, I have a question," asked Steadius. "If we are about to embark on this journey in search of the magical land of Corporate Utopia, shouldn't we have a planned approach with logical milestones that are signposted to clearly show us the way?" asked Steadius

"Yes, I agree!" whispered Associus in support of Steadius.

"Do not worry about a plan. Those things only slow us down,

and they only limit our potential to get there faster. Besides, I have the loudest voice and people are sure to follow me," shouted Dominus, who then reflected for a moment: *if only they knew that I also feared getting bored and becoming restless. Life would not be interesting if it was planned. Besides, I hate working to rules and thrive best under pressure and chaos.*

"But Dominus, if we cannot see where we are going, then how are we to prepare for a journey to achieve our vision of Corporate Utopia in the magical land?" argued Steadius.

"We need maps, compasses, tents, candles and matches." Steadius insisted. "For I value logic, order, routine, security and appreciation. Why is it that you do not value my contribution, Dominus?"

To reinforce his point, Steadius said, "I will be loyal to you and the community if I can fully understand the logic and rationale of the work that is to be achieved. I will work beside you diligently when I know what my role is in our quest for innovation. Until then, I have to say regretfully that I cannot follow and support you."

Steadius began to think: *I know that I fear change and insecurity and for the sake of my family, I cannot put them at risk of facing the 'evil spirits' that we will encounter on our adventure. I would much prefer to stay here where it is safe, warm and secure. I know that I have a need for certainty and routine. Why is life an eternal conflict for me?*

Steadius held his head in his hands. *If I trip and fall whilst on the journey, I'm sure to blame those that coerced me into this mess. I know that I have a tendency to hold grudges because people have told me that I have the memory of an elephant and I never forget.*

Perfectionus was waiting to speak. "Hang on, Steadius, maybe we can get more information about the journey. Maybe we can get Dominus to explain in greater detail the specific aims, objectives, tasks, milestones and the contingency plan if things don't work out," said Perfectionus calmly. "I will contribute my valuable time to conduct a risk assessment if required, as this will also give me certainty and security as we move along."

"Yes, I agree," said Associus.

"We need clear and logical plans before we can begin," said Steadius, as he rose to his feet and stood firmly, his arms crossed. "Yes, I agree with you as well," said Associus.

"We don't have time to plan. We must begin immediately!" Dominus pronounced sharply.

"Yes, I agree with you as well, Dominus," said Associus.

Associus thought to himself: *yet another sleepless night, but at least I'm with friends and everyone seems happy, especially Dominus.*

Perfectionus stood firm. "No, Dominus, until I have a clear and detailed plan that is accurate and correct, I will not put our valuable time and contribution at risk. We need to have it right.

Besides, there is only one way to do a job—the right way, first time and every time."

Steadius agreed. "Dominus, there is only one way to do a job and that is to plan your work and to work your plan. Without a plan, we are sure to be lost."

"Dominus, there is only one way to do a job and that is for us to talk about it as a team so that we can come to a consensus with peace, harmony and goodwill for all," said Associus.

"That's nonsense! There is only one way to do a job and that is my way! If you don't like it, then piss off!" said Dominus.

"Yes, I agree with you as well, Dominus," said Associus.

Again, Associus thought to himself: *yet another sleepless night. But what can I do to make Dominus happy and not create tension? He is, after all the leader, albeit self-appointed. Maybe Dominus is just a naughty little child who will sulk when he is not in the limelight. I wonder if his bad and inappropriate behaviour would be rewarded, like the squeaky wheel that gets the oil. I bet as a child he learned that by throwing tantrums, it guaranteed a way of getting attention from his parents.*

Perfectionus began to withdraw and reflect: *I hate it when people criticise me and my work effort, especially when I try to contribute common sense and factual information. If only they knew that I would start to lose motivation when chaos and disorder create stress in me.*

Looking away, Perfectionus continued to think: *this is becoming all too hard, besides I don't need this negative environment. I am already doing the best that I can. Why is it that I always think that people are criticising me?* He thought about his father who would constantly say things like, "try harder and be perfect, Perfectionus" or "you could have done that better, Perfectionus, maybe next time you'll get it right."

"It's okay, Perfectionus, I agree with you. You can always count on me to be your friend," said Associus, sensing and feeling that something was troubling Perfectionus.

Time passed and soon, Dominus, Associus, Steadius and Perfectionus were already wondering how their journey in search of the magical land of Corporate Utopia was going to end up.

Already, each of them had learnt so much about each other. Although they do not know it at this stage, this learning will assist them to create and maintain an ideal working environment on their journey to the magical land.

> What does your team need to know about managing the egos of different people in the workplace?

Go to the Innovation Hit List at the back of this book and consider how you could improve the workplace with what you have just read in this chapter.

SECRET NO.1

- Get commitment from all employees in developing an innovative working environment.

SECRET NO.2

- Develop innovative initiatives that are linked to key performance indicators.

SECRET NO.3

- Have a clear purpose and objective when creating an innovative working environment.

SECRET NO.4

- Identify timeframes and deadlines when undertaking initiatives or projects.

:>The Tablets

- Success and Learning

> *Never before in history has innovation offered*
> *promise of so much to so many in so short a time.*
>
> **Bill Gates**

That night, at the end of the first day of travel, Dominus, Associus, Steadius and Perfectionus sat calmly by the campfire chatting as the ambers slowly turned into grey ash.

" You know, already, this journey has been a real learning experience for me and we have only just begun," reflected Dominus. "I was reflecting on what happened earlier this morning and how we stumbled over the loose rocks on our path to uncover the instructions to reach the 'Tablets of Success'. I'm glad the previous exploration and reconnaisance group left their notes behind so that we can learn from their experiences."

"Apparently, they had turned upon one another because they did not value diversity within their team. All were murdered in their sleep, except one. They say that he took his own life after going insane trying to find the magic land of Corporate Utopia on his own," claimed Dominus.

He went on. "The messages from those tablets are firmly etched in my mind. I can recite the inscription that was on every one of the tablets of success!"

Dominus began reciting the etchings from the first tablet that focused on success secrets:

"As an innovation pioneer, you must ensure that there is a clear communication and consultative process within your team. Be sure to develop and support co-operation by providing clear expectations and defining the objectives of the task for your innovation team.

"As an innovation pioneer, remember to focus on productivity, that is, being effective and efficient, by setting clear parameters and working guidelines. Remember to establish clear outcomes of performance and to challenge the traditional paradigms of your team members."

"Dominus, I too recall those etchings, but from the second tablet," said Associus excitedly.

"Share that with us, Associus, my friend," Dominus urged. Associus began his recollection of the tablet:

"As an innovation pioneer, allow the thought processes of individuals to be expressed so as to create a motivating work environment. As an innovation pioneer, provide clear timeframes and develop the skills of your people. Remember to use reward and recognition to lock in good behaviour.

"As an innovation pioneer, consider the 'best fit' of a person for the task of developing strategies that allow people to adapt to change when working together. Create a collaborative but competitive working environment that is challenging."

"You have a good memory, Associus," responded Dominus whilst gently but firmly placing a hand on the shoulder of Associus.

"But not as good as mine, for I have the natural ability to retain information," boasted Steadius.

"Prove it then," Dominus challenged.

Steadius took a deep breath and explained, "The third tablet is based on pure logic, fact and reasoning."

"As an innovation pioneer, share your experiences and create opportunities for individuals to become positively committed to the quest. Ensure that your people have a collective input into problem-solving and decision-making in order to gain extra support.

"As an innovation pioneer, you shouldn't have hidden agendas. You should constantly look for better ways of doing things."

"You are absolutely 100% correct!" cheered Perfectionus as he ticked off the outcomes against his own mental checklist. "This is why I am proud that we have taken the time to etch our learning into our very own stone tablet so that others who follow in our footsteps can learn from us."

"I wonder why they murdered their team members later on in the journey?" Dominus said quietly.

"I have written a master copy so that I can reflect on the knowledge we gained whenever we enter into uncharted territory in the future," said Perfectionus.

Perfectionus continued, "I proclaim that our very own stone tablet will provide us with the certainty we need to overcome the challenges that are brought before us by the 'evil spirits of inner conflict'. "

"Hear! Hear!" Dominus, Associus and Steadius cheered.

"Read it out, Perfectionus, for all of us to hear!" Associus and Steadius urged.

Go to the Innovation Hit List at the back of this book and consider how you could improve the workplace with what you have just read in this chapter.

SECRET NO.5

- Have an identified 'creative hit list' of ideas that will allow people to focus on continuous improvement opportunities.

SECRET NO.6

- Identify roles and responsibilities when undertaking initiatives and projects in the workplace.

SECRET NO.7

- Develop proactive processes to build commitment towards allocated projects and initiatives.

SECRET NO.8

- Have a strategy to maintain the organisation's innovative and competitive edge.

∴ The Ponds

- Leaders and Followers

> *I believe in being an innovator.*
>
> **Bill Gates**

As the sun dawned on a new day of travel, the four pioneers commented on how the fog was beginning to thin and how the warm summer days were soon to be upon them.

"This reminds me of the morning when we came across one of our first challenges," exclaimed Steadius.

"What are you going on about?" questioned Dominus.

"The ponds of reflection. That was the first of the personal challenges that we had to overcome," said Steadius.

Associus jumped in with support for Steadius , "Don't you remember, Dominus?"

"Each of us was given personal insights from the ponds of reflection on what we have learnt as we journey to the magic land of Corporate Utopia," remarked Steadius.

"Ah yes, now I recall," said Dominus slowly. "We were all able to reflect on our leadership styles and approaches." He continued, "I recall my own personal ref lection on how I have developed to become a highly effective leader who will act as a positive role model for others. What I learnt was this: to be knowledgeable, to be fair but firm, and to be approachable."

"Remember, Dominus, effective leadership is the perception of the follower. You may perceive that you are doing a good job but it is the followers' perception that is reality," said Steadius.

Dominus nodded and thought for a while. "I need to develop good listening skills and to have confidence in myself and others. On occasion, I will have to remember to be supportive and provide positive feedback. I also need to learn to be patient and calm whilst defending and supporting individuals in my work environment."

"Excellent work , Dominus! Sounds like you had some very similar insights to myself!" gushed Associus. "I personally found that I have developed and grown in several areas, and can be a positive role model for others to learn from. I need to remember to consistently demonstrate fairness and equity with people at all times. As strange as it may seem, I now understand the importance of creating a work environment that is fun and lively, and yet at the same time, remaining professional by knowing what is going on."

"Makes logical sense to me, Associus. You just have to make sure that you are not all talk and no action," advised Steadius.

"Remember, effective leadership is the perception of the follower. You may perceive that you are doing a good job but it is the followers' perception that is reality," Dominus repeated what Steadius told him.

"I have analysed the following about myself," proclaimed Steadius as he took out his notes. I need to:

- Ensure that I am well-organised.

- Remain flexible but focused.

- Develop highly effective interpersonal skills.

- Be consistent with directions, instructions and decisions.

- Have knowledge of the task and job at hand.

- Constantly use good listening skills.

- Develop good communication skills that can be used upward, downward and across the workplace and team.

- Make sure I lead by example.

- Be unbiased (fair and equitable) and make sure that I don't play favourites.

"Again, you are all 100% correct. By the way, I liked the logical way you put your analysis across to us. Very succinct, almost to the point of being clinical," Perfectionus stated whilst cross-examining these findings against a mental checklist.

"Remember Steadius, effective leadership is the perception of the follower. You may perceive that you are doing a good job but it is the followers' perception that is reality," challenged Dominus a second time to overcome his insecurities.

Perfectionus thought: *if only I had a piece of paper! I would have been able to document this information for posterity.*

It was Perfectionus' turn. "I have learnt much about myself and how I can develop my leadership style and approach. Let me share with you my rationale and findings. I have to make sure I don't over-lead by interfering with competent and committed people. I must be conscious of giving recognition when warranted.

"I don't want to admit it, but I have to ensure that I have empathy with the people I work with. I need to demonstrate to them that I will back them up so that I may develop a reputation for being trustworthy."

He paused, then continued. "Leading by example is about working with integrity and having knowledge of the tasks that need to be done whilst remaining fair and equitable."

"Perfectionus, did you know that people thought you were anal-retentive when you led them in the old land?" scoffed Steadius.

Mhhh...was that what they thought? Perfectionus pondered.

"It appears to me, my friends, that we have all learnt so much about ourselves and the perception of reality as we progress towards the magic land of Corporate Utopia. I'm sure that our leadership styles and qualities will hold us in good stead in overcoming the 'evil spirits of inner conflict' that we are sure to encounter in future quests," Dominus said summarily.

"I firmly believe that it is the s e newly -found leadership behaviour and attitudes that have kept us from killing one another in our sleep like the previous exploration and reconnaissance group," observed Associus.

"Rest well, tonight, my friends," said Dominus smilingly.

> What does your management team need to know about being effective leaders in your workplace?

Go to the Innovation Hit List at the back of this book and consider how you could improve the workplace with what you have just read in this chapter.

SECRET NO.9

■ Get people to investigate opportunities for improving effectiveness and efficiencies within the workplace.

SECRET NO.10

■ Maintain structured communication processes to enhance open communication throughout the workplace.

SECRET NO.11

■ Have a positive working environment with minimal conflict between workgroups.

SECRET NO.12

■ Decision-making processes should reinforce fairness and equity.

∴ The Urns

- Persuading and Inspiring

Innovation is the central issue to economic prosperity.

Michael Porter

After many weeks and months of being on the journey, our four innovation pioneers were now beginning to self-actualise on their personal growth and achievements. They all observed an increase in confidence, leadership skills and team maturity within themselves and one another.

"Lunch is ready, my friends. Come and join me so that we can discuss our achievements," Perfectionus called out.

"Do you remember at the beginning when we made a list of our team values on a sheet of paper?" asked Associus.

"Yes, I recall how we described what we wanted in so many

words. I have now realised that it isn't about words. It is all about demonstrated behaviours," reflected Steadius.

"Perfectionus, do you still have a copy of our team values with you?" enquired Associus.

"Of course, Associus . It is my point of reference whenever I begin to doubt what I am doing and where we are along our path to the magic land. Would you like me to read them out to you?" responded Perfectionus.

"No," said Dominus bluntly. " Words are nothing more than ink on a piece of paper. I value only people who demonstrate their commitment to achieve the vision."

"No, wait!" Associus cried out. "I feel it is important for us to anchor our successes so that we can build upon them. Go ahead, Perfectionus, read them out for us all to hear."

"Okay, here they are," Perfectionus said as he unravelled the original document.

Perfectionus proceeded to read as he hammered his notes into the closest tree trunk for all to see in plain view. "As we learn and develop ourselves in search of innovation, we will encourage and support the innovation pioneer team values."

TEAM VALUES FOR PIONEERING INNOVATION		
Participation	Exchange of Skills and Knowledge	Dynamic
Personal Growth	Going Beyond the Boundaries	Trust
Action Orientated	Self Actualisation	Creative and Innovative
Contribution	Leverage and Synergise	Learnings
Community Orientated	Flexible and Fluid	Live and Behave the Values

"They are still only words," barked Dominus.

"Friends, what were the specific behaviours that we have observed that support these words?" exclaimed Steadius.

"It still sounds like nonsense to me," remarked Dominus. "Dominus, maybe we need to consider what we learnt from our experience when we finally unlocked the secrets at the clay urns," said Steadius patiently.

"Yes. I have the first of the secrets with me. Are you interested in recalling what they are?" invited Associus.

"Good idea," they chorused. But Dominus remained silent. He valued action and not words. He didn't have time for this. "It still sounds like nonsense to me," he mumbled under his breath.

"I have three scrolls, one from each clay urn. Let's sit calmly by the light of the fire and reflect for a moment," suggested Associus.

"I will sit by the fire because I am cold, not because I want to read words and feel good," scorned Dominus.

Perfectionus then said, "Okay, one each then, except for Dominus. I'll start.

The secrets from the first clay urn revealed that it is important as team leaders to use appropriate levels of communication and avoid jargon. It is also important to listen and not jump to conclusions. It is important to provide people with a central point of reference to help them understand the context of the message. Break the communication into logical stages, parts and sequences."

This makes a lot of sense, don't you think, Dominus?" said Associus, seeking harmony.

"It still sounds like nonsense to me," insisted Dominus.

Associus continued, "Always give people the big picture and get progress reports from your team. Get feedback to check their understanding and make sure you get acknowledgement from people by allowing questions and suggestions."

"You know, this makes perfect sense. I can now understand how some of our messages were misinterpreted, especially at the beginning of our journey," said Steadius.

"Hurry up, Associus, read out the next one! I'm fast losing my patience on these fluffy topics," challenged Dominus.

"Okay! Okay!" responded Associus. "The second clay urn revealed to us that it is important to use constructive, and not destructive, feedback and to make sure the information we provide is accurate and reliable. Always make sure that we use congruent body language and explain instructions clearly whilst being considerate of the pace and speed of message delivery."

"This is all good stuff," reflected Steadius.

"Sounds like nonsense to me!" stated Dominus.

"Dominus, your behaviour and actions towards us have been totally inappropriate. You know, your behaviour has a direct impact on ours," said Steadius.

"No, wait, Dominus! Maybe these are the 'evil spirits of inner conflict' that we need to learn to fight against in order to grow with abundance!" said Perfectionus.

Dominus sulked a little as Steadius read out the final set of secrets from the third clay urn. "Communicate clearly the scale and size of the task to your team. Reduce as many distractions and distortions as possible."

"I think we have all learnt that although a message is sent with positive intent, our 'evil spirits of inner conflict' often distort it or distract us from the true meaning," said Perfectionus.

"Because we are the early pioneers of innovation, let us develop our own set of secrets for other innovation seekers so that they may follow in our footsteps," proclaimed Dominus.

"Excellent suggestion!" they responded, in an open and honest manner. But they were surprised that Dominus agreed too. Maybe he did see the value of effective team communication after all.

Maybe the other exploration and reconnaissance group killed their team members as they slept because they all lacked patience and tolerance with one another, reflected Perfectionus.

What does your team need to know about effective communication?

Go to the Innovation Hit List at the back of this book and consider how you could improve the workplace with what you have just read in this chapter.

SECRET NO.13

■ Develop structured and standardised processes for decision-making.

SECRET NO.14

■ Be flexible in adapting to change that is caused by external or internal influences.

SECRET NO.15

■ Have initiatives and projects that positively support cost-effectiveness and efficiency strategies.

SECRET NO.16

■ Get commitment from your manager for developing an innovative working environment.

⠶The Spirits

- Good and Evil

Asking the right questions takes as much skill as giving the right answer.

Robert Half

Sitting by the warm campfire as the sun began to set on yet another interesting and challenging day, the discussions of our four characters turned to how they could control their own 'evil spirits of inner conflict'.

Each was becoming aware that their personal strengths might also be the foundation for their personal weaknesses.

Unusual as it was for Dominus, he managed to take the time to sit down and reflect over a meal of char-grilled pheasant and a goblet of very rough red wine that had been fermenting in his haversack during the journey. It must have been the wine that made him drop his guard.

"Well, let me tell you about me," said Dominus in his brusque and abrupt manner.

"I have come to realise that I am a person who is direct and forceful and who is driven to achieve wherever possible the perfect solution. I am a self-starter who enjoys a variety of tasks, including challenging and demanding ones. I also prefer to work alone and dislike being reliant upon the team and others."

Hesitantly, he continued, "Despite my sometimes aggressive approach, I am somewhat internally reserved and have an innate need to explore new projects, providing that I can see opportunity within a situation.

"I am exceedingly active and will show urgency in most situations. Because of this, I may bypass convention by being very strong-willed. Providing that things are going well, I'm also forward-looking."

Hearing this, the other pioneers were surprised. This is a first, thought Steadius.

"Dominus, I would like to hear what else you have learnt about yourself on this journey," said Associus.

Dominus went on to reveal. "I have discovered that I assume responsibility in all dealings. I am goal-oriented and a very strong decision maker. I sometimes seem too demanding, impatient and inflexible to others. I may seem to lack both sympathy and empathy.

This could intimidate some people. Whilst attention to detail is not my strongest point (having such a strong sense of dominance), I'm sure that if a result depends upon getting the facts and figures, I will force myself to do just that."

"Tell us more, Dominus!" marvelled Perfectionus.

"Well, I'm motivated by independence, both of the rules and of people. I also need room to move and the authority to act without constraint and to have my authority accepted. I have a continual need to win, to prove my ability and to be recognised as an achiever, such as may be seen in the power of my position," boasted Dominus.

"Dominus, that is an interesting insight to yourself. Would you like to hear a few words of how I would describe you?" asked Associus tentatively.

"Go ahead, Associus, you have caught me in a good mood and the red wine is just starting to warm my cheeks," exclaimed Dominus as he took a deep breath in preparation for the feedback.

"I would describe you by the following words," said Associus. "Driven, demanding, forceful, independent, opinionated, blunt, strong-willed, restless, anxious, active, energetic, probing and skeptical. A self-starter, you typically ask 'what' and 'when' questions."

"Thank you, Associus. Maybe this is where my 'evil spirits of inner conflict' come from," said Dominus.

"How did you come to that logical conclusion?" scoffed Steadius. Dominus went on to explain about his 'evil spirits of inner conflict'.

"I have also discovered that I have a natural fear of failure, being taken advantage of and losing control of my environment."

Turning to Perfectionus, Dominus ordered brusquely. "Give me a piece of paper so I can write a note to myself for the morning when this red wine wears off."

He continued, "I now understand that my personal development opportunities are to learn to pace myself better and to know when and how to relax. I need to be aware of the type of needs that other people have. I now have the understanding that everyone needs to interact with others at various times. I also need to be accepting of the importance of rules and protocols."

"Excellent work!" Perfectionus commented encouragingly.

"Now that I have told you about me, it is time that you tell me about you, Associus," challenged Dominus.

"Well friends, this is what I have discovered about myself since I began this journey," said Associus. "I am an independent individual who is outgoing and enjoys meeting a variety of people in varying environments and situations. I am socially competitive, verbal, persuasive and charming. I have the ability to put across and sell my own and others' ideas and concepts, optimistically and enthusiastically."

Associus paused before continuing. "I am not by nature aggressive or antagonistic towards others. I certainly enjoy popularity and the limelight, and will seek opportunities to obtain public recognition."

Always enjoying a captive audience, Associus elaborates. "I'm not naturally decisive and particularly dislike making harsh decisions which may make me unpopular. I dislike routine and repetitive work, and am often inattentive to detail. Although I'm a good starter at projects, I tend to leave the finishing and servicing to others."

"How true is that!" scorned Dominus.

Associus continued, "I may come across as being more direct and assertive than I really am, due to my high degree of verbal independence. I have a high degree of work energy—fast-paced, mobile, alert and variety-oriented. I'm also good at painting the big picture and creating optimism and enthusiasm in others."

"Tell us more!" encouraged Steadius.

"Okay," answered Associus, enjoying every moment of being the centre of attention. "I'm also motivated by popularity, independence, variety, change and money for a good life. I also enjoy being generous and will seek opportunities to promote my ideas and myself. I am sometimes socially competitive and will avoid, wherever possible, antagonistic situations."

"Associus, that is an interesting insight on yourself. Would you like to know how I would describe you?" said Steadius.

"Go ahead, Steadius, you have also caught me in a good mood, but not because of the red wine," Associus said as he sat down on a comfortable rock in preparation for his feedback.

"Associus, I would describe you as being independent, self- willed, verbal, active, optimistic, enthusiastic, self-promoting, friendly, gregarious, social, communicative, a quick starter, mild and non-aggressive. You also ask 'who' questions frequently," Steadius summarised in a logical and dispassionate manner.

Associus reflected for a while and then explained how his 'evil spirits of inner conflict' are now very clear to him. "I have a natural fear of rejection, isolation and being ostracised by the group. My personal development opportunities will be to learn to develop more organised, systematic approaches to doing things, including following through with what I set out to do and not lose interest after the first five minutes."

Drawing a deep breath of courage, Associus continued. "I have to develop an understanding of how and when to be more firm by dealing directly with less favourable situations and not to be driven by guilt. I need to be accepting of the importance of completing tasks and meeting deadlines with the set agreements."

"Excellent work!" Steadius pronounced.

"Well, now it is your turn to tell us about your personal learning, Steadius. The floor is yours," encouraged Associus.

Steadius stepped with some reluctance to the light of the campfire that was quickly fading. "I see myself as a steady, reliable individual with a great deal of patience and quiet tenacity. I am independent of both people and the rules but rarely antagonise others knowingly."

Reflecting, Steadius continued. "I realise that I am very stubborn and indeed, could well challenge the establishment if I feel that an injustice has occurred. It is important to realise that I am justice-oriented as opposed to rule-oriented. I am a hard worker who likes to get on with the job by taking a practical approach and will work at my own pace. I find that if others try to hurry me along, my reaction is likely to be one of quiet, but dogged defiance."

In his usual logical manner, Steadius added. "I am self-conscious by nature and some people may misinterpret my non-demonstrativeness and rather retiring demeanor as aloofness, but this is not truly the case. I am team-oriented. I have come to the realisation that I am a good anchor and mooring for any team that I am a part of. In regards to administration, I have the ability to cope with both routine and repetitive work though not necessarily at a low level."

Going into further detail, Steadius reinforced his point. "I don't need a great deal of guidance but I do require a clear understanding of the task to be undertaken. I now understand that I have a tendency to avoid decision-making, especially when it comes to harsh or unpopular decisions (particularly quick decisions), and disciplining others.

"I am a logical thinker and very often have good ideas. However, there is a tendency for me to keep these ideas to myself unless asked. I am capable of applying myself to most service and support roles, particularly if they are of a technical or practical orientation."

"Steadius, I must commend your logic and rationale as you talked about your learning whilst you have been in search of innovation. What else can you tell us?" asked Dominus.

Steadius went on. "I seek sincere appreciation and feedback for a job well done. I also need job security. I like to have time to assess situations before acting. I am wary of insincere praise and will seek genuineness in my peers and superiors."

"Perfectionus, how would you describe me?" asked Steadius. Perfectionus gathered his thoughts to deliver the following message. "Steadius, I would describe you as being kind, self-conscious, thorough, patient, independent, hard-working, loyal, sincere, indirect, non-demanding, dependable, mild, unassuming, stubborn, tenacious, administrative, practical, and persistent. You also tend to ask 'how' questions."

"Thank you, Perfectionus," said Steadius who went on to summarise that his 'evil spirits of inner conflict' are change and insecurity. "I now understand that my personal development opportunities will be to learn how to better handle the reality of unexpected and ongoing change. I need to be aware when to delegate to other people to achieve desired results and to understand how to be more assertive with people when taking charge of certain situations.

"I also need to accept the opportunity to grow by learning to do new and different things in a variety of ways—other than my own standard approach," reflected Steadius.

"Again, sound and solid findings with a good structure and conclusion," evaluated Perfectionus.

" What about you, Perfectionus? Are you prepared to share with us the findings on your personal development since we embarked on this journey?" challenged Dominus.

"I'll do my best!" exclaimed Perfectionus. "As always," laughed Associus.

Perfectionus stood tall and adjusted his clothes as his shadow, cast by the flickering flames of the campfire, fell against trees lining the forest.

He then proceeded to unravel the neatly-folded notes that he had made on this quest and read from them. "I see myself as a systematic, precise thinker and worker who tends to follow procedure s in business life. I tend to proceed in an orderly, predetermined manner. I am precise and attentive to detail, rarely antagonising work members consciously and I typically act in a highly tactful and diplomatic fashion."

Perfectionus continued. "Most of the time, I will demonstrate a good sense of timing and shrewdness in making the right decision.

Being an extremely conscientious person, I work painstakingly on my projects and strive for accuracy. I seek constantly to establish and maintain standards.

"I enjoy standard operating procedures, with no sudden or abrupt departures from the standards, unless I had time to think through all the implications of such a change. I prefer to share responsibilities in areas where I don't have total knowledge or expertise and may at times, look for reassurance from others."

His three companions listened patiently and nodded from time to time. Encouraged by the positive and non-critical feedback from his peers, Perfectionus added, "I don't like spending excessive time away from my home and family. I find that dealing with the unfamiliar and unknown is stressful. I need assignments that are precise and are of a project management nature. I also need to have access to high levels of expertise, knowledge, technical people and physical resources to have confidence to move forward."

Perfectionus elaborated further. "For me, detailed explanations are essential at times of change as I must have full knowledge, understanding and the logical rationale behind the changes.

"Due to the very high standards that I demand of myself, I prefer to work with fellow specialists and experts rather than generalists. I could be very systematic, precise and proficient, with a demand for a similar attitude from co-workers and team members."

"Perfectionus, you amaze me with your ability to turn human

behaviour into a logical science. Well done! Is there anything else you would like to share with us?" Associus asked.

"Yes, get on with it." By this time, Dominus was getting bored with all this talk and detail.

"Yes, Associus," said Perfectionus. "Let me continue with my well-documented notes. I am a person who is motivated by clarity of work expectations and the security of the situation. I normally need to feel accepted by the organisation but not necessarily to feel like a part of it.

"Reputation, accuracy and preciseness are very important to me. I often find myself seeking the opportunity to work alone or on the periphery of a team because I have a high personal need to have access to details, instructions and guidelines."

"Are you ready for some feedback?" yawned Dominus in his typical challenging manner as he refilled his wine goblet with the rough red nectar.

"Only if it is specific, factual and logical," said Perfectionus. "Okay, I'll be stretching my natural behaviour on this one, but I will give it a go," grunted Dominus. "I see you as accurate, precise, detailed, skeptical, probing, systematic, logical, deliberate, analytical, wary, self-conscious, reflective and non-aggressive. You ask 'why' and 'when' questions frequently."

"Thank you, Dominus. Your feedback provides me with the clarity of what my natural fears are—insecurity and criticism of performance," said Perfectionus.

Perfectionus continued reciting his findings from the neatly scripted notes. "I have learnt the following about controlling my 'evil spirits of inner conflict.' I need to learn to develop a greater tolerance for conflict and human imperfection. I also need to develop realistic approaches to prevent and minimise both.

"I also need to be more aware of the importance of direct communication. I need to discuss my viewpoints with others. I have to develop an understanding of the different types of talents and interest levels of individuals, which can be helpful in achieving desired objectives."

After a short pause, he continued, "I have to be accepting of true self-esteem and the importance that I have as a worthwhile person in my own right, rather than only for what I do."

"Let us erect a monument which describes those essential elements of feedback that have assisted us to become aware of our 'evil spirits of inner conflict,'" suggested Associus.

"That's right. By giving and receiving feedback about what 'we know about ourselves' and about what 'others know about us,' we have created an open communicative environment, and reduced the number of blind spots and errors in judgements that we may have had of ourselves previously," exclaimed Steadius.

"Sounds like a complete waste of time to me!" slurred Dominus. On that comment, they turned to one another with stunned looks of surprise and then bellowed with laughter.

What do your workplace leaders need to know about providing positive and constructive feedback to workplace employees?

Go to the Innovation Hit List at the back of this book and consider how you could improve the workplace with what you have just read in this chapter.

SECRET NO.17

- Have interesting and challenging jobs as a result of workplace initiatives and projects.

SECRET NO.18

- Develop a structured process that ensures that the correct innovation initiative is selected.

SECRET NO.19

- Create shared ownership between employees and managers on initiatives or projects.

SECRET NO.20

- Put in place effective management practices that ensure all initiatives and projects will have a positive impact in the workplace.

꞉꞉The Pillars

- People and Passion

The measure of our future success and happiness will not be the quality of the cards we are dealt by unseen hands, but the poise and wisdom with which we play them. Choose to play each hand to the best of your ability without wasting the time or energy it takes to complain about either the cards or dealer or the often unfair rules of the game. Play both the winning and the losing hands as best you can, then fold the cards and ante up for the next deal!

Joe Klock

By now, our innovation pioneers were fast realising that 'different is different' rather than that 'different is wrong'. They also realised that, as they went on the quest for innovation, the answers lie deep within each of them. All they needed to do from the beginning was to open their minds and hearts to be ready to receive the solutions.

They have thus arrived at the magic land of Corporate Utopia.

Highly motivated, the innovation pioneers immediately set to work applying the lessons gained on their journey to the construction of the land of innovation.

After many seasons, communication and co-operation have now become commonplace and are ingrained within the culture of the land. The land is now well-populated with creative and dynamic people who are competent and committed to supporting the community quest for innovation.

To celebrate the third anniversary, the townsfolk decided to name their magical land of Corporate Utopia. Dominus proclaimed on behalf of the townsfolk that this settlement would now be known as Nirvana.

With pride in his voice, Dominus continued. "Nirvana is chosen because it means a transcendent state in which there is neither suffering, desire, nor sense of self, and our towns people can be released from the effects of karma and the corporate life cycle of death and rebirth. But remember my friends – there are no short cuts in Nirvana. It represents our final goal!"

At this point, Associus rallied for support by cheering. "Three cheers for Nirvana. Hip, hip...hooray! Hip, hip...hooray!" The townsfolk cheered in unison and reaffirmed the name 'Nirvana.'

Teams were then formed. They were to etch onto pillars the precise elements that would create and maintain a motivating environment, one that supports each team's vision and values. These are to be known as the 'pillars of motivation.'

The first pillar focused on motivation. On it, the inscription read:

- Provide recognition and appreciation to people within your community and team.

- Provide people with challenging and interesting projects and tasks.

- Create satisfaction by allowing people to have control, autonomy and responsibility for outcomes.

- Pay people their worth and let them get on with it.

- Create a working environment that allows people to achieve their personal goals.

- Provide people with feedback on the results of the completion of the task delegated to them.

- Say 'thank you' more frequently.

"I never thought I would say this, but I have finally come to accept that it is okay to say 'thank you' and to provide people with positive praise and feedback," said Dominus humbly to his companions.

He went on to explain. "I used to think that saying 'thank you' and giving encouragement was a sign of weakness. I think this is a 'throw-back' to what my father used to say to me: 'try harder, be perfect, Dominus. You are stupid and lazy. You should have done that better, Dominus'. "

Attempting to analyse the situation, Dominus continued. "My father always used to reinforce certain ideas in me such as not to trust anyone, or to 'stick it to him or her before they stick it to you.' I now know that this statement is also a throw-back to what my grandfather said to my father. I would guess that this was heavily influenced by their upbringing and environment in the limestone quarries of their village." Smiling, he let on proudly that his father was once an imperial guard for 20 years.

A stunned silence ensued. "Let's look at the second pillar of motivation," someone suggested, breaking the awkward silence.

> The second pillar focused on the development of workplace passion. It proclaimed the need to:
>
> - Create situations where people can see positive outcomes for their efforts.
>
> - Provide people with the appropriate recognition that satisfies their personal needs.
>
> - Provide people with relevant rewards and payments.

"You know, although I understand these behaviours, I think I need to better understand the processes behind them, in order to create a better working environment. This could be the 'evil spirits of inner conflict' that I may need to control," said Steadius.

Steadius went on to explain. "I was once told by a wise person that as soon as I moved away from dealing with the technical tasks and on to dealing with people, there is an increased chance that I will become more stressed. This wise person added that one can always switch off a machine but it is always challenging to switch off a person."

"You're right, Steadius. Machines are logical and predictable whereas human beings are not. On saying that, if I can better understand what motivates individuals, then I can develop higher levels of empathy and respect for them," stated Perfectionus. "I may also begin to understand what motivates me. This is why, for me, the information on the third pillar is of high personal value."

The pillar focused on mentoring. It read:

- Provide people with clarity and purpose about their duties and roles within the community and the team.

- Allow people to develop and grow by giving them different and interesting tasks.

- Acknowledge the achievements of your team, especially the newcomers in it, so as to lock in 'good behaviour'.

- Provide people with challenges by delegating responsibilities to them for which they have great interest.

Despite agreeing with some of the ideas and concepts stated earlier, Dominus scoffed. "I still can't come to terms with accepting this fluffy stuff."

He pondered to himself: why am I having difficulty accepting this?

Steadius smiled and tried to comfort Dominus.

We are all different, Dominus. Do not kick yourself because you value achievement of task over interaction with people. Stay positive and focused. The key is to realise that your personal 'evil spirits of inner conflict' is normal and lives within each and every one of us. Your answer could lie on the fourth pillar."

"Go and check it out!" urged Steadius.

With some reluctance and arrogance, Dominus approached the final pillar which was titled 'enlightenment'. He did not want to be described as arrogant, although he had often been told of this trait of his in the past

He quietly read the information to himself:

- Create development opportunities for people within your team.

- Create situations where people enjoy what they do by allowing them to do what they want to do instead of what they have to do.

- Create working environments that allow for efficiencies to occur and tell people of the improvements.

- Allow people to take on tasks of responsibility so they get a sense of achievement.

> - Consider situations where people can be put into new positions that align with their personal values.
>
> - Provide clear goals and deadlines that people can work to.

As he walked away from the last pillar, Dominus whispered to himself. "Today is the day that I will leave behind my redundant behavioural traits."

Turning to his companions, Dominus proclaimed. "Today, my friends, we are no longer innovation pioneers. From this day on, we are innovation heroes!"

The townfolk united and roared. "Three cheers for the innovation heroes! Hip, hip...hooray! Hip, hip...hooray!"

What does your team need to know about changing ineffective patterns of behaviour to embrace change?

Go to the Innovation Hit List at the back of this book and consider how you could improve the workplace with what you have just read in this chapter.

SECRET NO.21

■ Get feedback from internal or external customers on their needs when undertaking workplace projects and initiatives.

SECRET NO.22

■ Develop communication strategies to reduce the fear of change in individuals and teams when going through the change process.

SECRET NO.23

■ Be proactive in keeping people informed on matters to reduce levels of frustration in individuals and teams.

SECRET NO.24

■ Create financial rewards and incentives to reinforce positive workplace behaviour.

⋮⟩ The Poles

- Innovation and Paradigms

A wise person will make more opportunity than he finds.

Francis Bacon

Daily routine is now commonplace in Nirvana, the settlement of Corporate Utopia.

There had not been a single report of murder or homicide in the community. Not even a single incident of anyone being stabbed in the back by others nor of self-inflicted wounds of people falling onto their own swords.

This is because everyone recognised the importance of respecting and valuing diversity, and of creating trust and rapport throughout the entire community.

Maybe this is how the previous exploration and reconnaisance group failed. If they had overcome their 'evil spirits of inner conflict', they would also have been able to enjoy being part of the living and thriving environment now.

Everyone in the prosperous community of Nirvana now understands that the quality of their thinking will have a direct impact on the quality of their future. With this in mind, they brainstormed what the next few years could bring.

They were fast coming to the realisation that they were running the risk of becoming complacent and limiting their personal and professional growth as a result of staying in their comfort zones.

Once again, Dominus made the first move. "We must now begin to look for new opportunities and possibilities. We need to be recognised as diamonds and not dinosaurs by our peers. Most important, we need to be kept informed of trends that are on the horizon to ensure that we have a variety of interesting projects to be involved in."

" Yes, we also need to make sure we provide everyone with personal reward and remuneration," said Associus eagerly.

"Already I'm bored and need a new challenge. For I know that if I don't challenge myself, then I will become disruptive and will begin to antagonise those people who are in their comfort zones," stated Dominus.

"I agree. We need to have a plan so that we can take action on a proven path to challenge the boundaries for innovation success," rallied Steadius.

"I don't have time for plans. Let's just do it!" said an agitated Dominus.

"Haven't you learnt from past situations, Dominus, about your strengths and weaknesses?" queried Associus.

"Dominus, what did you learn from the ponds and pillars about success and achievement?" Steadius probed.

"Yes, yes. I hear you loud and clear," Dominus said impatiently.

"Yes, but are you listening, Dominus?" confronted Associus.

"Do I need to mention the urns and tablets as well, Dominus?"exclaimed Perfectionus.

"I'm best at giving advice, not taking it. I'll have to practise my effective listening skills," commented Dominus humbly as he realised his mistake.

All four laughed in unison.

"We need to make sure that we can all win as much as we can so as to create a positive environment that fosters camaraderie and cooperation," said Associus cheerfully when the animosity appeared to have dissipated.

"My friends, I recall the writings that appeared on the wisdom poles as we entered the settlement of Nirvana. It read: 'The land you are entering is the same as the land you left behind. If you do not change, then this land will be the same as the last'. "

Reinforcing his point, Associus added. "How do we make our land an inspiration for others to respect and admire?"

"Well, let me tell you, my needs are simple. Provide people with progress reports and updates to make sure we are on-track or off-track, and develop an environment of trust with people by using effective leadership," pronounced Dominus confidently as he came forth, ready for action.

Looking at Associus, he said encouragingly, "Associus, my friend, come forward and tell us your personal needs."

"I agree that we need to challenge the boundaries of innovation and that we need to create opportunities for people to seek and clarify our goals and objectives. Secondly, we must reach agreements with our people and then use our leadership abilities to demonstrate support for them," replied Associus.

"I fully agree with your logic and rationale," stated Steadius.

Steadius went on to support the need to challenge the paradigms of individuals, teams and the community. "I think that your findings are well-founded and based on solid research. Your findings are similar to mine. Let me share with you what I think is vital. It is vital that everyone knows what the innovation initiative is before getting into the 'doing' part of the process."

"Excellent work, Steadius. I want to add to your findings with greater detail and specification. This will support my hypothesis," said Perfectionus.

Perfectionus continued. "I have personally documented and categorised work behaviour according to certain criteria. My report shows the following:

> • Treat all team members with equality and equity.
>
> • Don't single out certain people as your favourites.
>
> • Make sure to keep your perceptions in check.
>
> • Be aware of your actions and consequences as a leader.
>
> • Clearly outline the rules of operations with your team.
>
> • Provide opportunities to clarify questions and concerns.

In unison, all four characters said, "Let's capture our thoughts and place them on our own wisdom pole so that others can learn from our personal and team experience."

"I think I had better do this. It will be a good way for me to tame the 'evil spirits of inner conflict resulting from my lack of patience and tolerance'. They appear to have control of me at the moment," said Dominus sheepishly.

He continued. "Associus, pass me the chisel so that I can start immediately. I want to be able to go to sleep with my mind at peace tonight, without the thought of my life being in danger."

Go to the Innovation Hit List at the back of this book and consider how you could improve the workplace with what you have just read in this chapter.

SECRET NO.25

- Have a record of success by putting 'quick wins on the board' when undertaking new projects and initiatives.

SECRET NO.26

- Encourage innovative thinking that supports the organisational goals and objectives.

SECRET NO.27

- Get active involvement from employees and management to get 'buy-in and support' for initiatives and projects.

SECRET NO.28

- Use initiatives and projects as a way to capture and ignite (utilise) the corporate intelligence.

⸪ The Stones

- Abundance and Lack

> *People who have attained things worth having in this world have worked while others idled, have persevered while others gave up in despair, have practised early in life the valuable habits of self-denial, industry and singleness of purpose. As a result, they enjoy in later life the success so often erroneously attributed to good luck.*
>
> **Anonymous**

The four innovation heroes are now well on their way to identifying and understanding themselves and others. However, their thirst for innovation and improvement was just beginning to be quenched.

As they shared a meal together, they began to realise that each of them was so vastly different yet similar in so many ways.

Dominus reached across to his tatty leather backpack and took out his trusty wine goblet that had also endured the journey in search of innovation. He proceeded to pour himself what he proclaimed to be his best vintage of nectar to date. As he did so, he commented, "I'm beginning to become bored and restless."

"Strange, I'm just beginning to enjoy the routine that we are having," stated Steadius.

"You know, I have come to realise that I'm motivated by certainty and systems. There is nothing better than waking up and knowing that you had the day planned," said Perfectionus.

"Oh no, I couldn't stand that. Variety is the spice of life for me," said Associus.

"I'm with you, Associus!" bellowed Dominus as he paced around the table and finally placed his backpack in the shade of a young citrus tree.

Steadius interrupted by challenging him. "You know, Dominus, this reminds me of when we were confronted by the troll as we approached the gates to the magic land of Nirvana."

"What are you babbling on about, Steadius?" said Dominus in a brusque manner.

Steadius exclaimed. "Do you remember, before we could enter, the troll asked us to prove our worth by playing a simple game?"

Associus recalled how the troll screeched out the challenge: "Are you ready to win as much as you can?"

The troll had provided each of the four characters with a stick and a stone, and told them to each stand in one corner of the village square.

The troll then told them not to talk to one another and to hold above their heads either a stick or stone (whatever they decided they were going to do).

"I'll never forget the rules of the game. As always, I have noted them down. It reminds me of the necessary types of behaviour needed to overcome the self-destructive forces of the 'evil spirits of inner conflict' when we have to operate as a team," said Perfectionus.

"Well hurry up and read them out, Perfectionus. My patience is fast wearing thin," commanded Dominus.

Perfectionus cleared his throat and read aloud.

RULES OF THE TROLL GAME
You will be remunerated by your demonstrated behaviour with brass razus in accordance to the payoff schedule shown below:
PAYOFF SCHEDULE
If 4 sticks are shown in the village square, you all lose 100 razus each.
If 3 sticks are shown in the village square, those three people each win 100 razus. If 1 stone is shown in the village square, that person loses 300 razus.
If 2 sticks are shown in the village square, those two people each win 200 razus. If 2 stones are shown in the village square, those two people each lose 200 razus.
If 1 stick is shown in the village square, that person wins 300 razus. If 3 stones are shown in the village square, those three people each lose 100 razus.
If 4 stones are shown in the village square, you all win 100 razus each.

"You know, Dominus, I couldn't believe how you reverted to your old ways and how your 'evil spirits of inner conflict' controlled you on that day," jested Associus.

"Yes, yes, no need to remind me. It is my natural thought that when I hear the word 'win,' then that means there is automatically going to be a loser. I will tell you right here and now that there is no way that I am going to be seen as a loser to anyone. The good thing is that I know that I have a natural fear of failure, of losing control and of being taken advantage of," said Dominus. "It is like a candle being lit with a match. It must be my fear of not succeeding."

"I know that you like a good challenge, Dominus, but in this case, your strategy of constantly holding high your stick constantly made us win nothing but lose much," said Associus.

"Yes, but the rules of the game clearly and simply state to win as much as you can and I won 300 brass razus," argued Dominus.

"But at what expense? You may have won but your behaviour caused the remaining three of us to lose 100 brass razus each," Steadius shot back.

"Altogether, we won a total of zero razus, nothing, zilch, not a single brass razu," said Perfectionus as he reviewed his checklist.

Associus reinforced the point. "We were being tested by the troll who was evaluating and assessing what we learnt about controlling our 'evil spirits of inner conflict' as we headed towards our magic land of Nirvana."

"At one point, the troll even offered us the single opportunity to openly discuss what our actions were going to be before holding high the stick or stone," recalled Steadius.

"I specifically recall that we agreed that if we each held up a stone, then we could all win 100 razus each," said Perfectionus.

"Yes, that's right. We could have walked away with 400 razus, instead of nothing at all," cried Associus.

"Dominus, my friend, why did you say one thing but then do another?" said Steadius mockingly.

"It does nothing but create distrust, greed, back-stabbing, conflict, resentment, communication breakdown and political game-playing," said Associus.

Dominus defended himself. "The rule was clear: win as much as you can."

He then thought to himself: *these 'evil spirits of inner conflict' have a good hold on me today. It is difficult to shake off these old, disgusting and redundant behavioural traits.*

"Maybe what we observed was just a symptom and not the cause. I now value highly the importance of having clarity of common goals and purpose before undertaking any activity as an innovative team," stated Steadius. "Well, you know what they say, quality input equals quality output. In this case, it was garbage in, garbage out."

"It was a good thing the troll allowed us to repent against our faults so that we could clearly demonstrate what we have gained from this experience," thought Associus.

"Dominus, what have you learnt about winning from this simple game of sticks and stones?" Steadius wanted to know.

Dominus stepped forward. "Although I'm reluctant to admit my own failings, I have learnt that it is important to develop an environment of trust with people by using effective and appropriate leadership styles and approaches."

Deflecting the focus off himself, Dominus asked, "What have you learnt, Associus?"

Associus was quick to remark. "Well, upon reflection, I have learnt to create opportunities for my people to clarify task goals and objectives."

"Hmmm...that makes good logical sense. For me, I have learnt I must ensure everyone knows what the tasks are before getting into the 'doing' part of the process," said Steadius.

"Now, for the correct answer!" boasted Perfectionus. From the silence came a roar of laughter.

"Go ahead, Perfectionus, my friend. As you always do, give us the correct response!" chuckled Dominus.

As he adjusted his glasses, Perfectionus looked at his notes and murmured four points.

- Make sure you keep your perceptions in check.

- Be aware of your actions and consequences as a leader.

- Clearly outline the rules of operations with your team.

- Provide opportunities to clarify questions and concerns.

"As always, my friend, you are 100% correct!" Steadius said to much laughter.

"Let us create a monument and call it the 'Stone of Achievement' so that our current and future community members can learn what we have learnt on our journey to the magic land of Nirvana.

"How about placing the Stone of Achievement - 888 paces from the gate to where the troll is? This way, future innovation heroes can learn from our experience," suggested Associus.

"Why, we had to find out the hard way. Let them suffer! We had to endure the challenges, and all kinds of pain and suffering. They should go through it as well," Dominus said insistently.

Quietly, calmly and confidently, Associus reaffirmed his point. "Dominus, life doesn't have to be a competition all the time. Think of the game 'tug-of-war'. It can only be played if you choose to pick up the rope."

"I have to start to learn to think before opening my mouth. As hard as it is for me to admit it, you are right, Associus. If we all work together, we will all get a far greater result. We need to lead by example for other people who are entering our magic land," said Dominus reluctantly but willingly.

Reinforcing his words with action, he continued. "I now know how we can all 'win as much as we can'. Can you please pass me the masonry chisel and hammer again, so I can get to work on our Stone of Achievement?" asked Dominus politely.

What does your workplace need to know about teamwork and synergy?

Go to the Innovation Hit List at the back of this book and consider how you could improve the workplace with what you have just read in this chapter.

SECRET NO.29

■ Have department leaders at all levels 'walk the talk' to act as positive role models.

SECRET NO.30

■ Have your leader 'walk the talk' to act as a positive role model.

SECRET NO.31

■ Have input from the team to develop commitment, accountability and responsibility.

SECRET NO.32

■ Get department leaders to reinforce and communicate the necessity and benefits of being innovative and competitive in the marketplace.

:>The Keys

- Time and Space

> *Few ideas are in themselves practical. It is for want of imagination in applying them that they fail. The creative process does not end with an idea—it only starts with an idea.*
>
> **John Arnold**
>
> *Massachusetts Institute of Technology*

On the way back from erecting the Stone of Achievement outside the gates, our innovation heroes decided to rest their tired and weary legs at the local water-hole as the sun began to set in the autumn sky. Each began to reflect on what challenge the troll would set them as they re-entered the settlement of Nirvana. The troll had given them a satchel of seven keys.

Each key opened one of seven different doors and beyond each door was the answer to how to gain commitment and support for all innovative initiatives for centuries to come.

The troll had given them precise and detailed instructions on how to focus their thinking in preparation for this next challenge.

"Perfectionus, do you recall what the troll said?" Steadius asked.

"Yes, I actually wrote it down. Each key is colour-coded to match each door, and each key has a specific function.

When opened with the correct key, the information behind each door will be interpreted by the person who is the holder of that key to innovation," recited Perfectionus.

Dominus interrupted. "I also recall reading from the instructions that came with the satchel that the seven keys to innovation are essential for fast and effective thinking, thinking that would foster an environment of immediate results with and through people."

Associus added, "That's right. There are seven metaphorical keys that the holder can use to indicate the type of thinking that is to be used. The analogy is 'take the key, open the door and step into that specific environment to effectively think.' "

Again, Dominus interrupted enthusiastically, "Yes, these thinking styles are to be used proactively rather than reactively, and must never be used to label people."

"They will make an effective alternative to the traditional debate and argument method we sometimes used in the old community which often stifled innovative thinking!" Steadius pointed out.

"Before we begin to open the doors to innovation with the seven keys, I would like to quickly review the instructions on each of the functions that came with the seven keys to innovation," said Perfectionus.

He proceeded to read from his notes the brief descriptions of the thinking functions.

Blue Key	What information do we need
Red Key	What does your instinct tell you
White Key	Investigate the merits of innovation
Orange Key	Consider the hazards of innovation
Gold Key	What choices do you have
Green Key	How are you going to take action
Purple Key	What resources do you need

"Excellent recital as always," commented Associus.

Associus continued. "I can now understand clearly how individuals and teams can contribute under any of these key thinking functions, even though they may initially support the opposite view."

"That's right. Valuable judgemental thinking has its place. But in this case, it is not allowed to dominate the thinking environment," stated Dominus decisively.

Steadius added, "The seven keys to innovation encourage everyone within the team to be supportive and collaborative by examining and discussing various situations together."

"Let us put them to excellent use by identifying how we can gain commitment and support for innovation within our community," suggested Associus.

"Excellent. I'll go first by taking the Blue Key to open the door that will provide us with all the critical information needed to gain commitment and support for innovation within Nirvana," said Dominus.

Focusing on the **Blue Key**, they listed the following insights they have gleaned from their journey to Nirvana:

- What is the vision/mission of developing innovation within the magic land?

- How can we link the innovative initiatives to performance indicators?

- What is the scope, objective and purpose of creating an innovative and forward-looking organisation?

- What are the identified timeframes and deadlines?

- What is the short list of ideas that could create innovation?

- What are the roles and responsibilities to facilitate innovation in the workplace?

- How can we develop and maintain commitment to the identified innovation initiatives?

"Wow, this is powerful stuff and we didn't even argue or, should I say, I didn't even argue!" said Dominus.

"Let me go next!" said Associus as he stepped up to grab the Red Key to open the door.

Associus went on to say, "This Red Key will provide us with what our instinct tells us to do to gain commitment and support for innovation within Nirvana."

Focusing on the **Red Key**, they agreed on the following:

- We need to be innovative to maintain a competitive edge.

- It is useful to improve effectiveness and efficiencies within the magic land.

- The pursuit of innovation will provide us with a structured thinking process that will allow us to have open communication.

- A collective effort to pursue innovation will reduce the amount of conflict that we have within our workgroups.

- Focusing on innovation will reduce the 'loudest voice wins' syndrome.

- Our decision-making process will be greatly improved.

"You know, this is the first time that I actually feel that what I have said has been valued by the three of you. Normally, it's the loudest voice that gets heard," said Associus.

"You are right," Dominus agreed humbly.

"I think I'm next in line," said Steadius in his usual logical and structured manner.

Steadius leaned forward and placed his hand in the satchel to remove the White Key that would open the door to reveal the benefits of gaining commitment and support for innovation within Nirvana.

Focusing on the **White Key**, they discussed the merits of what they have learnt on their journey to the magic land of Nirvana. They were able to identify and acknowledge that:

- Innovation creates flexibility—the community can implement various initiatives that support one other.

- Innovation also gains commitment and support to bring about cultural change.

- An innovative environment will create interesting and challenging jobs and initiatives.

- Innovation in the magic land will support cost-effectiveness and efficiency initiatives.

"It's a miracle! We haven't argued in the past 15 minutes!" exclaimed Steadius.

"The seven keys to innovation are excellent. They are certainly opening the doors to opportunity," said Dominus.

Perfectionus stepped forward to remove the fourth key to innovation—the Orange Key. This key would open the door to the words of caution on gaining commitment and support for innovation within the working community.

Focusing on the Orange Key, the four innovation heroes discussed the risks of what they had learnt on their journey to the Nirvana.

Quickly and easily, they acknowledged the following:

- There is a possibility of picking the wrong innovation initiative.

- There may be a lack of shared ownership within the magic land to support the innovation initiative.

- If badly managed, the innovation initiative may have a negative impact on future initiatives.

- There may be a lack of a proper needs analysis on and external stakeholders for the identification of goals, objectives and scope of the innovation initiative.

- There could be a fear of the change that would be brought about through innovative initiatives.

- If there is insufficient communication, people could become frustrated as they are not being kept informed.

"Well, I always thought looking at negatives was wrong. But without considering both sides of the equation, I may miss vital information," said Associus.

"Absolutely! It's a bit like having perfect vision in hindsight!" exclaimed Dominus.

"It looks like it's my turn again," said Dominus as he removed the fifth key to innovation.

The **Gold Key** opens the door to the set of choices for gaining commitment and support for innovation within the working community. The four innovation heroes quickly and easily concurred on the following:

- Build in financial reward mechanisms for both individuals and team.

- Get some quick wins to develop an innovation (paradigm shift) culture.

- Develop fresh approaches to achieving goals and objectives within the magic land of Corporate Utopia the settlement known as Nirvana.

- Involve all stakeholders in the innovation process in order to get 'buy in' to support initiatives.

- Stimulate corporate intelligence by getting people involved.

- Get leaders to 'walk the talk' and act as role models.

- Obtain input from the team to develop commitment to the whys and hows of all innovation initiatives.

- Create opportunities to reinforce the importance of sustainable competitive advantage within the magic land.

- Create opportunities to think of alternative approaches and avoid the risk of just being busy 'doing,' instead of thinking.

- Gain government funding to support innovation initiatives in the magic land.

- Develop outcome-focused initiatives for which the results can be easily measured.

"I'm starting to value the fact that we understand how one another works and thinks," said Dominus, to everyone's surprise.

"It must be a radical and new concept for you, Dominus. It's called teamwork," laughed Associus.

"Okay, only two more keys to go," said Steadius as he firmly grasped the Green Key that would open the door to the strategy and actions required to gain commitment and support for innovation.

Focusing on the **Green Key**, the four innovation heroes discussed the strategies of implementation whilst they were on their journey to Nirvana.

They concluded the following:

- Develop and/or incorporate innovation into the strategic plan with clear goals, objectives and key performance indicators.

- Develop a list of tasks with clear milestones.

- Develop relevant individual formal and informal reward and recognition processes.

- Celebrate wins to reward good behaviour and use the opportunity to promote the benefits and outcomes of the innovation initiative to those within and outside the organisation.

- Develop clear job descriptions for accountability towards supporting innovation initiatives.

- Conduct regular educational and promotional events on innovation for internal and external customers.

"All right, I am now seeing how the game plan for innovation is starting to come together," Steadius said slowly. Looking at Perfectionus, he said, "This leaves the final key to innovation for you to select and use, Perfectionus."

On that prompt, Perfectionus shook the contents of the satchel out to reveal the Purple Key that would open the door to reveal the physical and human resources required to gain commitment and support for innovation.

Focusing on the **Purple Key**, the four discussed and reflected on the roles that they and other innovation seekers had undertaken on the journey to Nirvana.

They concluded the following:

- General managers must take the initiative to regularly review existing vision and mission statements to include innovation.

- The heads of departments must develop area business plans in consultation with frontline managers to identify innovation initiatives with measurable key performance indicators.

- The frontline managers must implement and monitor innovation initiatives in consultation with team players.

> • The team players must take action, be personally committed and continually support all innovation initiatives within the workplace.

"All that remains now is an empty satchel and a wealth of learning that could be passed on to the next generation of innovators. They will then be able to follow in our footsteps to master innovation," proclaimed Steadius excitedly.

Dominus, Associus, Steadius and Perfectionus have now truly mastered innovation. They have learnt much about themselves and others on this journey to Nirvana.

They are...heroes!

You may also be interested to know that the myth of the previous innovation exploration and reconnaissance group whose members killed one another was simply just that—a myth.

It was later learnt that they merely lost their way. Getting back on track, they then followed the trail by picking up the clues left behind by Dominus, Associus, Steadius and Perfectionus.

However, when they reached the gates to the magic land of Nirvana, they were stuck outside in the freezing cold of night and the devastating heat of the day for over twelve months. This was because they could not solve the problem set by the troll. This meant that, until they resolved a number of issues within their dysfunctional team, they would not be allowed to enter the magic land of Corporate Utopia.

One day, however, the y stumble d on the solution to their problem—it was inscribed on the Stone of Achievement erected by Dominus, Associus, Steadius and Perfectionus.

For them, their quest for innovation was now over.

What does your team need to know about applying the seven keys to innovation?

Go to the Innovation Hit List at the back of this book and consider how you could improve the workplace with what you have just read in this chapter.

SECRET NO.33

■ Create the time and space to think of alternative approaches.

SECRET NO.34

■ Find out how to obtain government funding that supports your current innovation initiatives and projects.

SECRET NO.35

■ Have initiatives and projects that are easily measured and have clearly defined outcomes.

SECRET NO.36

■ Have a strategic plan with clear goals, objectives and key performance indicators.

⠶The Truth

- Attributes and Attitude

The greatest danger for most of us is not to aim too high and miss it, but to aim too low and reach it.

Michelangelo

Resting by a moonlit stream, Dominus appeared to be mesmerised by the dancing moonbeams as they reflected off the ripples of running water. A strange silence seemed to be holding the four innovation heroes hostage.

Associus was the first to break the silence. "I have come to the realisation that leadership is primarily about having a positive mental mindset and then about having a set of specific skills. If people trust and respect me as a leader of innovation, they are sure to follow," said Associus in an attempt to create some conversation.

Dominus was unusually relaxed and calm, as if a mystical charm had been cast upon him. "Associus, I agree with you, my friend. When I reflect on past leaders whom I admire and respect, there appears to be a consistent set of characteristics."

"What do you mean?" queried Steadius.

"I have worked for some idiots in the past, and I have worked for some idols in the past," stated Dominus as he snapped free from the hex and became his natural self. "The idiots totally lacked passion, inspiration, sensitivity and empathy, determination and commitment, honesty and integrity. I have no time for these fools."

"I agree, Dominus. There is no substitute for a leader who is firm, fair and consistent. Especially when it comes to making decisions and the ability to communicate with people at different levels," said Steadius supportively.

"As innovation heroes, we need to understand the townsfolk of Nirvana so that we can communicate our vision of innovation effectively. It is vital that we understand the science of human behaviour," said Associus decisively.

"Yes, manipulation is good," stated Dominus.

"Well, Dominus, negative manipulation may win you the battle, but will it win you the war on innovation?" asked Steadius.

"Maybe you would like to consider that leadership is the ability to influence others positively and with respect," posed Perfectionus.

"No, the best form of leadership is with this piece of rough-cut citrus branch that I have in my hand," joked Dominus as he whipped the sapling with his left hand.

Steadius thought to himself: *it is good to see that Dominus is in fine form and back to his natural antics.*

"As innovation heroes, we need a high level of emotional maturity. Brains will help us, but it's our ability to rise above adversity to reveal the natural leader within that counts," said Associus.

"What rubbish are you talking about now?" challenged Dominus. "Dominus, take heed of what I'm about to say for this information applies directly to you. You must control your 'evil spirits of inner conflict' inside the gates of Nirvana," said Associus firmly.

Dominus sat by himself, sulking slightly yet still engaged in Associus' philosophies of touchy-feely leadership and psycho-babble. "Controlling your emotions is vital if we are to have people follow us on the continued quest for innovation in Nirvana,"

Associus explained patiently. "We must manage the townsfolk whom we meet on a day-to-day basis. We must identify and have empathy for other people's emotions and feelings."

"Sounds like nonsense to me," said Dominus.

Stunned looks appeared on the faces of all the innovation heroes, except that of Dominus. He was in total denial.

"Show them the wrath of a rough-cut citrus tree, that's what I say!"

"Bear with me, Dominus," said Associus calmly. "Think about how you could positively motivate yourself and manage your emotions through self-awareness."

"Craaaaaaaaaaaap!" yelled Dominus in his defence.

Perfectionus stepped forward into the conversation. "That is right, my friends. By developing a high level of emotional maturity, we can be assured to be effective. Our demonstrated behaviours are sure to rub off on the townsfolk of Nirvana."

Steadius interjected, adding some interesting information. "If children learn from adult s, then adult s must surely learn from other adults. As innovation heroes, we have a duty and responsibility to increase stability and harmony, and improve social relationships. At the same time, we should act to reduce stress and potential conflict situations that may arise."

"Basically, it comes down to an individual's values of ethics and integrity," said Perfectionus.

"That is right. I once heard … " Associus started to say, but was interrupted mid-sentence by Dominus.

"Here we go...blah, blah, blah..." taunted Dominus impatiently. Associus disregarded Dominus' childish outbursts. He guessed that these outbursts were the result of Dominus feeling threatened by concepts of love and compassion—both of which he never received from his parents when he was young.

Frowning and looking firmly at Dominus, Associus said, "Okay, all I wanted to say was that ethics are the rules of the game and integrity is how you personally play the game."

"As the founding leaders of innovation in Nirvana, we all have a personal obligation to act as positive role models for the townsfolk. They look to us for direction and clarity," said Perfectionus.

Steadius nodded. "I agree. We need to have a thorough understanding of the values that are connected to ethical behaviour. We must all have the personal commitment and motivation not to be swayed or distracted by our 'evil spirits of inner conflict.' "

"As individuals, we must never compromise on our own values, which are closely aligned to that of Nirvana's. Our townsfolk expect us to walk the talk whilst creating an atmosphere of peace and goodwill for all," said Associus.

"Pass me that citrus branch, Associus. I am going to instill some ethics and integrity into the townsfolk right now!" said Dominus determinedly as he strode out of range of the flickering firelight of the campfire.

"Quickly, my friends, let us work on a personal development plan for Dominus so that he does not undo our good work with his ignorance and arrogance," urged Steadius.

Perfectionus started making a list of the positive behavioural traits that are to be expected of an innovation hero—today and for centuries to come.

Positive and expected behavioural traits of an innovation hero

- Be compassionate by acknowledging people on a regular basis and remind yourself to say the words "thank you" and "I appreciate your effort" on a regular but not predictable basis.

- Respect and support the values of Nirvana even if they differ from your own personal set of values.

- Remain honest, fair and impartial when dealing with the townsfolk in order to develop a high level of trust and rapport.

- Remain open-minded, optimistic and approachable; support the other innovation heroes on their quest to foster innovation in Nirvana.

- Always remain gracious, humble and sincere; maintain a high level of emotional maturity.

- Be firm, fair and consistent in all of your actions and decisions with the townsfolk of Nirvana.

Sound travels great distances in the still of the night. Extending beyond the radius of the firelight haze to where Dominus rested on a rugged but comfortable rock outcrop. He had had time to reflect on his own as the other three innovation heroes were making the list of positive behavioural traits. Running through Dominus' active mind was the script that he wrestled with daily.

His father had instilled these words into him when he was just a small child: "Dominus you can't take the whole world to the psychiatrist. Emotional maturity has to start from within. It cannot be given to you. It is a decision and action that must be made by you and no one else."

With that, Dominus re-entered the bright comforting environment of the campsite to reveal to the other innovation heroes his insights.

What can you do to get input and commitment from the people in your team?

Go to the Innovation Hit List at the back of this book and consider how you could improve the workplace with what you have just read in this chapter.

SECRET NO.37

- Break down tasks and milestones with clear timelines when undertaking projects and initiatives.

SECRET NO.38

- Have informal reward and recognition processes for individuals.

SECRET NO.39

- Develop formal reward and recognition processes, such as performance appraisals, for individuals.

⠶The Fusion

- Responsibility and Accountability

Creativity is worth nothing unless the corporate intelligence of the organisation is captured and ignited. Remember, creativity is the idea and innovation is the action to that idea.

Greg Kinnaird

Manager and Author

(Organisational Development / Learning and Development / Talent Management)

Anew dawn was approaching, not only in the fine land of Nirvana but also in the minds of our four innovation heroes. They were now starting to realise that they and the people must not be complacent. For they understand that the killers to maintaining an innovative environment of Nirvana are expansion, achievement and effectiveness.

As they sat soaking up the morning sunshine of this new day in the village square, the conversation turned towards the future direction of Nirvana.

Dominus was fast becoming impatient and bored about how routine and predictable life was becoming in Nirvana. Letting out a great sigh, Dominus said, "I'm bored."

"What are you saying, my friend?" asked Associus.

"I'm bored. I need something to challenge my mind and spirit. I know that I will soon start to become a negative influence on the townsfolk with my natural arrogance and aggressive manner if I'm not occupied with worthy tasks," Dominus said sulkily.

"Well, maybe you need to have a bit more control of your 'evil spirits of inner conflict," said Steadius.

"Steadius is right, Dominus. For a person like you who is such a big control freak, the only person you can't control is the one that is inside your mind. It is indeed the irony of ironies," Perfectionus commented matter-of-factly.

"All I'm saying is this. We must channel our thoughts, energy and efforts to maintaining an innovative culture here," Dominus said.

"Have you not noticed that since the celebrations were over, the townsfolk have started to become agitated?" said Dominus. Continuing quickly before any of the others could interject, he said, "My friends, I have observed that cracks are starting to appear in the fabric of our society. We must manage the behaviour of the townsfolk so that they are focused on good and not evil."

Associus affirmed what Dominus said. "Actually, I've noticed that the conversations of the townsfolk have centred around the same few questions in the past few weeks."

"Specifically, what type of questions?" queried Perfectionus.

"Well, the classic questions that we have seen before in other working environments, such as what is the goal and direction of Nirvana, what is my specific role and the role of others in Nirvana, and what is the process we are going to use to achieve the goals and roles that we set out to achieve?" Associus answered.

Steadius supported Associus' observation. "Yes, the root cause to every societal uprising is that community leaders have not taken the time to clearly communicate the goals, roles and processes for building unity to their townsfolk."

He suggested the following course of action. "Let us sit down and discuss. We should come up with a plan for Nirvana to maintain its innovative culture."

"No, I don't have the time and patience to plan. Let's take action!" urged Dominus.

"No, we must consult with the townsfolk to get their buy-in if we are to capture and ignite corporate intelligence," said Associus.

"Yes indeed. If we don't plan, then how can we work together in a structured manner? Lack of planning will only cause confusion and will certainly add fuel to the fire of uprising," urged Steadius.

"No, we must look for evidence of how capturing and igniting people's desire to foster innovation has been done before. That way, we can benchmark our success against our plan. It is important that we have key performance indicators so that we can monitor and evaluate our progress as we go forth to maintain the competitive and innovative edge of Nirvana," pleaded Perfectionus.

"Perfectionus, have you ever stopped to wonder why people call you 'Mr Logical?' " asked Dominus antagonistically.

"Dominus, I can see that your evil spirits have caused you to get out of the wrong side of the bed this morning," quipped Associus.

"Yes, yes, you are right. As much as I hate to admit it, I do apologise, Perfectionus," said Dominus humbly.

Steadius tried to focus the heroes' attention. "For us to maintain a level of professionalism, we need to send out a congruent message to the townsfolk. Remember, we are their innovation heroes and they look to us for direction, guidance, and support."

"Dominus, this is an opportunity for us to utilise the powers that were unleashed from the seven keys to innovation!" rallied Associus. "Do you still have the satchel that was given to us by the troll as we entered Nirvana?"

"Yes, it is right here in my backpack, next to the well-fermented nectar and my trusty wine goblet," said Dominus.

"Well, place the satchel on the rock ledge next to you, pour yourself a goblet of nectar and be prepared to have patience for the next thirty minutes as we use the seven keys to innovation to seek wisdom and enlightenment," instructed Associus tactfully.

Perfectionus stated, "Our objective is to identify and discuss what we can do as innovation heroes to sustain the innovative climate here at Nirvana."

"Hurry up, let's start! I'm already getting frustrated with all this talking and it has only been three minutes!" barked Dominus.

The other three innovation heroes looked at one another across the limestone table and rolled their eyes in unison.

"Dominus, you start," instructed Associus.

Dominus reached into the ragged satchel with his large and rough left hand and extracted the **Blue Key**.

As Dominus was doing this, Associus reinforce d a point. "Remember, there are seven metaphorical keys that the holder can use to indicate the type of thinking that is to be used. The idea is to take the key, open the door and step into that specific environment to effectively think with the power that is possessed within that specific key."

Dominus removed the **Blue Key** from the satchel, opened the metaphorical door, and entered into that specific environment with an open mind to effectively think.

"Remember, Dominus, with the **Blue Key**, you need to focus on what relevant information is needed for Nirvana to maintain its competitive and innovative edge," Perfectionus reminded him.

"Okay, enough already. Do not tell me what to do. I am not an idiot," barked Dominus as he focused his mind.

Dominus steadied his restless mind and breathed calmly. "Well, this key is guiding me to say that we need to know how to be innovative and to know where Nirvana wants to be in the future."

"Excellent, Dominus," said Perfectionus approvingly.

"Okay then, you're next, Associus," instructed Dominus in an authoritative tone.

Associus reached into the satchel and removed the **Red Key**. He immediately opened the metaphorical door with it, and entered into that specific environment with an open mind to effectively think with the power that was possessed within the **Red Key**.

"Remember, Associus, with the **Red Key**, you need to focus on what your instinct tells you about Nirvana and how it may maintain its competitive and innovative edge," reinforced Perfectionus.

Associus steadied his active and optimistic mind to breathe calmly. "There are a number things that this key is guiding me to say," said Associus. "Firstly, the townsfolk are excited with the future prospects of Nirvana. They appear to be in full support of maintaining the competitive and innovative edge of Nirvana.

There is a feeling of success, pride and personal power that is coming from the townsfolk as they embark on this new quest. There are a silent few who have a need for rewards and incentives for their efforts."

"Good work, Associus," Perfectionus concluded, smiling.

"Would you like to go next, Steadius?" asked Associus gently, in his usual caring and diplomatic manner.

Steadius reached across the limestone tabletop that was getting warmer as the morning sun rose over the village square.

Taking the satchel and opening it, he reached in and removed the **White Key**. Slowly, he opened the metaphorical door with it and entered into that specific environment with an open mind to effectively think with the power that was given by the **White Key**.

"Remember, Steadius, with the **White Key**, you need to focus on what merits there are for Nirvana as the townsfolk continue their quest for innovation," reinforced Perfectionus.

Steadius allowed his naturally sceptical mind to be open, optimistic and positive as he began to breathe in a relaxed rhythm. "There are a number of things that this **White Key** is guiding me to say," said Steadius. "I am very surprised at my findings, my friends. I have a long list. Perfectionus, do you have that trusty piece of paper and writing instrument with you?"

"Yes, it is right here, next to my slide rule," said Perfectionus. Dominus rolled his eyes and smiled knowingly at Associus. Steadius continued. "Write down the following, Perfectionus.

The **White Key** is guiding me to say that the merits to Nirvana are as follows."

- There will be endless benefits for Nirvana if it maintains its competitive and innovative edge.

- We will be ahead of the competition.

- We will meet the challenge of the values and guiding principles that we have established for Nirvana.

- We will have success and make an impact.

- Nirvana will become a leader in the busy marketplace it operates in.

- It will be both enjoyable and satisfying to be associated with a winning team.

- Nirvana could win global awards if it maintains its competitive and innovative edge.

- As a community, we will take pride in our contribution to the greater good and eliminate any bad faith.

"Steadius, I'm amazed at your level of positive optimism. These keys to innovation are doing more than opening doors for you. They are opening and expanding your mind," said Associus.

"Would you like to go next, Perfectionus?" asked Steadius as he slid the open satchel across the table and in the direction of Perfectionus.

Perfectionus put down his writing instrument and neatly folded his notes, placing them in a chronological order into his file. Adjusting his sitting position on the limestone perch, Perfectionus reached into the satchel and removed the **Orange Key**. Holding the key tightly, Perfectionus prepared his mind to effectively think with the power that was possessed within the **Orange Key**.

"Remember, with the **Orange Key**, you need to focus on the hazards and obstacles that the people of Nirvana will face as they are on the quest to become innovative," reinforced Dominus.

Perfectionus' naturally analytical mind found this an easy task to embrace. His conservatism helped to identify several things. "There are a number of things that this **Orange Key** is guiding me to note down," said Perfectionus.

"Associus, please take my writing instrument and a clean sheet of paper from my file and help me make notes," Perfectionus asked politely.

"Who, me?" asked Associus anxiously, thinking that Steadius would be better at this task.

" You'll find fresh paper next to my b o ok on calculus and logarithms," said Perfectionus, as if he hadn't heard Associus.

Again, Dominus rolled his eyes and smiled at Associus with a knowing look. They both laughed and shook their heads.

Perfectionus started to dictate his findings as Associus furiously scribbled the notes. "The **Orange Key** is guiding me to tell you that the hazards for the people of Nirvana are as follows."

- There will be chaos and distraction as we start our quest for innovation in Nirvana.

- Our quest could ultimately create an inclusive and/or an exclusive environment and we will need to value those people who aren't naturally innovative.

- Red tape will stifle innovation in Nirvana.

- We must ensure that our quest is not seen as a 'flash-in- the-pan' initiative; we as innovation heroes need to support the townsfolk for sustainable development to occur.

- There is a danger that Nirvana will stimulate innovation initiatives but will have the wrong people working together to achieve them.

> - As innovation heroes, we need to be open and responsive to those townsfolk who may challenge our paradigms and our limited thinking which may be brought on by our very own 'evil spirits of inner conflict.'
>
> - Politics, ego and too much male testosterone could distract and keep people away from Nirvana's innovation initiatives.

"Perfectionus, you amaze with your logical ability to put concepts into a precise dot-point format," said Dominus good-humouredly.

"Dominus, it is your turn again to reach into the satchel to use the seven keys to innovation," said Perfectionus in reply, as he proceeded to proofread the scribbled notes that Associus made on his behalf.

"Throw the satchel over to me," commanded Dominus. Perfectionus tied the loose cord around the opening of the satchel to secure its content, a textbook-perfect reef knot, and then passed the bag to Dominus.

Dominus tugged hard at the string and opened the bag. He extracted the **Gold Key** with the gracefulness of a raging bull in a glass-blowing factory.

Again, Associus reinforced the message. "Remember, there are seven metaphorical keys that the holder can use to indicate the type of thinking that is to be used. The analogy is 'take the key, open the door and step into that specific environment to effectively think with the power that is possessed within that **Gold Key**."Disregarding what Associus had said, Dominus opened the metaphorical door and entered into the specific environment with gusto, and an open mind to effectively think.

"Remember, Dominus, with the **Gold Key**, you need to focus on potential opportunities and choices that Nirvana can embrace on this new quest," Perfectionus reminded him.

"Ssssssssshh, stop telling me what to do!" barked Dominus. Dominus again steadied his restless mind and breathed calmly.

"There are a number of options that this **Gold Key** is presenting me," said Dominus a while later. "First, we need to put together a think-tank so that we can capture the intelligence of our townsfolk. Second, we must counter the things that could stifle innovation at Nirvana. Third, as innovation heroes, we must be transparent with all our findings, and lastly, Nirvana must get global recognition for being innovative."

Associus supported and reinforced these findings by adding: "That's right, we could expect to see an increase in community satisfaction as innovation becomes part of the social fabric at Nirvana."

"The counterpoint to this, Associus, would be that we may lose the basics of what Nirvana is all about because we could get 'innovation overload,' " said the natural cynic in Steadius.

"That's right. We could end up losing a lot of money, and hence create a politically unstable environment in Nirvana. If we win a globally recognised award for being an innovator, it will all go downhill from there," Perfectionus argued.

"Well, it looks like Dominus is not the only the person who has been affected by the 'evil spirits of inner conflict' during the evening," commented Associus in his subtle manner.

Humbled by Associus' comment, Steadius and Perfectionus tried to rein in their evil spirits.

"Okay, you're next, Steadius. Go get a key from the satchel," said Dominus cordially to break the awkward silence.

Steadius prised apart the opening of the soft leather pouch to remove the **Green Key**.

He opened the metaphorical door with it and entered into that specific environment with an open mind to effectively think with the power that was possessed within the **Green Key**.

"Remember, with the **Green Key**, you need to focus on the specific action needed for implementing the opportunities arising from Nirvana as it fosters innovation," reinforced Perfectionus.

Steadius allowed his naturally cynical and evaluative mind to be open to the steps required to make innovation happen in Nirvana. He began to breathe calmly and focus his thoughts.

"There are a series of steps and activities that the **Green Key** is guiding me to explore," said Steadius.

"Let me list them for you, Perfectionus. Hand me that sheet of paper that you have in your file," instructed Steadius. He wrote the following as he spoke:

- Step 1
  Conduct market research with the internal and external customers of Nirvana. This will need to be done with the support of the innovation heroes and the co-ordinators of specific initiatives of innovation. Together they can scope out what is need to be achieved in the next 12 weeks.

- Step 2
  Research what other towns have done before in the past to be innovative. The townsfolk of Nirvana will also need to do this with the support of the innovation heroes and the co-ordinators of specific initiatives of innovation. Together they can map out what needs to be achieved in the next 12 weeks.

- Step 3
  Bring in experts from other towns to identify the habits that are stifling innovation in Nirvana. Do this with the support of the innovation heroes and the co-ordinators who are the key points of contacts. This can be done within 24 weeks.

- Step 4
  Have experts from other towns facilitate a series of sessions with every region and located within the settlement of Nirvana to identify areas where the people can become

innovative. Do this with the support of the innovation heroes and the co-ordinators who are the key points of contacts. This can be done within 36 weeks.

"You are a natural at converting broad concepts into a succinct and logical plan. It is a gift that I can only hope to achieve in another lifetime," said Associus.

"Well, my view is that planning is worth nothing unless it is implemented," scorned Dominus.

"Perfectionus, there is only one key left in this satchel and I think it has your name on it," quipped Associus as he pushed the bag across the table to Perfectionus.

Perfectionus dipped his well-manicured fingers into the bag and then dusted off the lint that had attached itself to the **Purple Key**.

"Remember, Perfectionus, with the **Purple Key**, you need to focus on the resources we need to get the job done," said Dominus.

Perfectionus closed his eyes for a while and then said, "There are five things that we need in order to achieve our objective for Nirvana to foster innovation and maintain its competitive edge," stated Perfectionus.

Pausing, he then summarised. "We need time and money. We also need committed leaders and townsfolk, and the discipline to follow through. The **Purple Key** is telling me that creativity is worth nothing unless the collective intelligence of Nirvana is captured and ignited. It is important to remember that creativity is the idea and innovation is the action to that idea."

"Well done, Perfectionus! You appear to have seized the essence of what is needed to ignite the fuse as we continue in our quest for innovation at Nirvana," said Associus supportively. "Dominus, fill up your goblet with that sweet nectar so that we can propose a toast and drink to good fortune and health."

Each of the innovation heroes took turns to drink from the well-used and slightly stained goblet as they made a pact to maintain Nirvana's innovative edge.

Then suddenly, "Quick pass me a cloth! I spilled some sweet nectar and it will stain the limestone table!" said Perfectionus anxiously.

With that, they all looked in the direction of Perfectionus.

As unusual as it was, Dominus put his arm around Perfectionus and said, "You have such an eye for detail, you can do the paperwork that is needed for this quest."

They all laughed.

What are your low, medium and high priorities to starting to be at your innovative best today?

Go to the Innovation Hit List at the back of this book and consider how you could improve the workplace with what you have just read in this chapter.

SECRET NO.40

■ Celebrate, reinforce and reward the benefits and outcomes of project and initiative successes.

SECRET NO.41

■ Have clear job roles and descriptions with identified accountabilities.

SECRET NO.42

■ Conduct regular educational and promotional events on project updates to internal customers.

⋗The Blueprint
- Prioritising and Planning

It is not the plan that counts; it is the planning.
Having a plan is excellent but you need to qualify
your thinking as you move into the next phase.

Greg Kinnaird

Manager and Author
(Organisational Development / Learning and Development / Talent Management)

Towards the day's end, the innovation heroes started to discuss the importance of prioritising the specific actions to be undertaken as they continued on their quest for innovation in Nirvana. Over dinner, the conversation turned to some of the concluding comments that Perfectionus had made earlier that morning.

"Perfectionus, I'm interested to hear your thoughts on what we have to do to sustain our quest for innovation in Nirvana," said Dominus.

"Well, Dominus, I can see that I have caught you in a good mood and at a time when you have the patience to listen to what I have written down," said Perfectionus.

"Just as long as you don't dribble and waffle on with irrelevant information that leads us nowhere," scoffed Dominus as he looked across to the others.

"As it just so happens, I have made a set of detailed notes of what I see as the top ten driving forces that will support innovation in Nirvana," said Perfectionus as he handed each of the innovation heroes his notes.

"You have neat handwriting," commented Associus, wanting to support and encourage Perfectionus.

Dominus took the opportunity to tease him. "How long did it take you to do this? Obviously, you mustn't have a life!"

They all laughed.

Ignoring him, Perfectionus scanned through his neatly-scripted notepad and read from his notes. "The top ten driving forces currently supporting innovation are as follows."

1. A structured communication process that enhances open communication throughout the town.

2. A decision-making process that reinforces fairness and equity.

3. The flexibility to adapt to change that is caused by both external and internal influences.

4. The processes that are in place to keep people informed so as to reduce levels of frustration among the townsfolk.

5. Leaders who understand the importance of 'walking the talk' so as to act as positive role models for others.

Pausing, Perfectionus looked at Dominus. "Are you still with me?" He wanted to keep Dominus engaged in the conversation.

Dominus nodded. "Yes, I am. I can see your logical rationale and I do support what you are saying," said Dominus with a newfound respect for Perfectionus' sharp mind.

Perfectionus looked down at his notes. "Okay, I'll carry on reading out the remaining top five driving forces that are currently supporting innovation in Nirvana."

6. A strategic plan with clearly-defined goals, objectives and key performance indicators.

7. A formal reward and recognition process for individuals such as the Nirvana performance appraisals.

8. A clear set of job roles and descriptions with identified accountabilities.

9. A team of innovation heroes who regularly review the existing business vision, mission statements and business plans.

10. Innovation heroes who had input and developed business plans with key performance indicators in consultation with the townsfolk.

"Good work, Perfectionus!" cheered Dominus.

Perfectionus thought to himself: *that was unusual. It's rare that Dominus would give praise to a task well done. It is not normally in his nature to do so. Normally, I have to operate from the perspective that no news is good news when I deal with Dominus.*

Associus and Steadius also looked perplexed at the comment that Dominus made. "Dominus, it looks like we have truly caught you in a good mood," commented Associus.

"Yes, well..." said Dominus. "Don't get used to it."

"Ah, yes. This is the Dominus that we have all come to know, and love," said Associus in good humour.

"Well," Steadius said after no one spoke for a while. "My friends, I have also been having some thoughts of my own since we used the seven keys to innovation this morning. There are five primary restraining factors that are holding us back at being our innovation best here in Nirvana."

"Well, let's hear what they are then," ordered Dominus.

Steadius continued. "How I see it is that as innovation heroes, we need to take immediate action on the following items. It is critical for Nirvana to have an identified 'hit list' of ideas that focuses people on continuous improvement opportunities. We also need to get active involvement from the townsfolk and other centres of influence to get buy-in and support for the initiatives and projects that we will be rolling out."

Observing that no one spoke, Steadius said, "Do you follow me?"

In unison, the rest nodded their heads in agreement.

Steadius continued with his train of thought. "We need to make sure that we create the time and space to allow for the thinking of alternative approaches. This includes looking for opportunities to seek funding from sources that support our innovation initiatives and projects. This funding could either be in the form of cash or in-kind contributions."

"Great idea!" enthused Associus.

"I have one more final point," said Steadius as he prepared himself for his concluding comment. "We must conduct regular educational and promotional events on innovation projects and give information updates to the townsfolk and customers."

"I can see your logic, Steadius. I fully agree. I am beginning to value that planning does play a role in fostering an innovative environment," said Dominus. "I wrestled with my 'evil spirits of inner conflict' during the day and prepared a written list of actions that I need to control.

"Don't look so stunned, my friends. I may lack patience, but I do not lack the ability to see that when a job requires planning, I'll set myself the task, stretching my natural behaviour, to get the paperwork done," Dominus stated with conviction.

Everyone looked in awe as Dominus removed from his tattered backpack a neatly folded piece of paper. He felt proud.

Perfectionus was highly respectful of the extraordinary efforts that Dominus went to. Interestingly, it could be observed that the paper shook ever so slightly as Dominus held it in his hand to begin his speech. He wouldn't admit to fear but his instinctive and encoded body habits were communicating it loud and clear to the other three innovation heroes.

"I agree with much that has been said by Steadius, so I will only add what I see as the next set of actions that are required. It is vital for Nirvana to have the following."

- Commitment from all townsfolk in developing an innovative environment in Nirvana.

- Identified time frames and deadlines when undertaking initiatives or projects.

- A positive work environment with minimum or no conflict among workgroups.

- A structured and standardised process for decision-making.

- Interesting and challenging jobs as a result of workplace initiatives and projects.

- A structured process that ensures that the correct innovation initiative is selected.

"Are you still with me, Perfectionus?" enquired Dominus with subtle antagonism.

"Actually, I'm still analysing this incongruency of behaviour. It is seldom that we see you utilise such sound logic and fact. To be honest, you have impressed me, Dominus," said Perfectionus graciously.

"It is as if I'm listening to something that I may have written. Are you sure that you didn't get your wife or children to write this?" asked Perfectionus with a newfound respect for Dominus because of his discipline to set his mind to the task.

"Don't get too used to this," said Dominus. "I seriously had to wrestle with my 'evil spirits of inner conflict' to do this task. So I expect you all to listen up to what I have to say." He proceeded to read out the final two points listed at the bottom of the page.

- We must have townsfolk act as leaders. They will reinforce and communicate the need and benefits of being innovative and competitive in the local and global marketplace.

- We need innovation initiatives and projects that can be easily measured and have clearly defined outcomes.

"Even I am impressed! Good work, well done!" said Steadius.

"Let's have a group hug!" rallied Associus.

"You stay on your side of the table, Associus, and I stay on mine," said Dominus quickly as he scrunched up his neatly printed notes into a ball in preparation to throw it into the waste bin.

They all laughed, except for Dominus, who was dead serious about not wanting a group hug.

After a moment of awkwardness and silence, Steadius cleared his throat and took the opportunity to put across his views on what had to be achieved once the action plans of Perfectionus and Dominus were implemented throughout Nirvana.

"My friends, I have an announcement to make," said Steadius. "First of all, let me say that I agree with what the both of you are suggesting. Most importantly, I agree with the priority of the actions that must be taken. I would like to suggest that once these have been achieved, we can implement the following. Although they are of lower value to what you have identified, I think that they are still of some value to Nirvana.

"To me, it is important for Nirvana to have a clear purpose and objective when creating an innovative working environment. We must also ensure that there is a proactive process of building commitment towards allocated projects and initiatives. This includes developing and implementing a strategy to maintain Nirvana's innovative and competitive edge.

"Can you see my logic and where I'm coming from?" queried Steadius so as to create discussion and dialogue with the other innovation heroes.

Associus responded immediately. "Crystal clear. We are with you." "I'll proceed then," said Steadius as his conviction for the ideas he was about to put forth grew. "The townsfolk of Nirvana need to proactively investigate opportunities that will lead to improved effectiveness and efficiencies, especially where they lead to increased revenue and reduced expenses," said Steadius slowly. "Because the townsfolk see us as innovation heroes, we need to develop methods that will encourage innovative thinking and we must always remember to 'walk the talk' ourselves.

"The key factors that we are looking to get the townsfolk's input on pertains to commitment, accountability and responsibility," concluded Steadius.

Looking around, Steadius remarked. "Associus, I see that you are deep in thought. It is most unusual for you to be so quiet. Normally you are bursting out of your skin with an abundance of ideas and enthusiasm," said Steadius.

"I was just thinking how aligned my thinking is with yours. Every time I was just about to add a suggestion, you brought it up yourself," marvelled Associus.

"Well, you know what they say, don't you? Great minds think alike," said Perfectionus.

Associus then commented that he did have a couple of points to add if Steadius had finished.

"Go ahead, Associus, I'd be delighted to hear your ideas," said Steadius encouragingly.

Leaning forward onto the dining table, Associus cleared the plates and glasses that were in front of him and said, "This may sound soft, but I truly believe that we need to have regular celebrations to reward the townsfolk. This will provide us with the opportunity to sell the benefits and outcomes of successful projects and initiatives.

"I would also like to get personally involved in training the townsfolk so that they can competently use the new processes and systems being implemented as a result of Nirvana's business improvement projects. Especially the new innovations in regards to the tools of the trade that our townsfolk use on a daily basis.

"There is one final recommendation that I would like to make, and that is that we, the innovation heroes, must use a consultative approach when we monitor our projects," said Associus.

At that point, Dominus interrupted and said, "Dealing with people, having patience and effective listening skills are the basic foundation of my 'evil spirits of inner conflict.' I can see many a fine wrestling match coming up, my friends. All of those will be with the demons deep inside my head."

"Dominus, be assure d that you have our full support and friendship for when you do," said Associus.

What do you need to do to be an innovation pioneer or hero?

Go to the Innovation Hit List at the back of this book and consider how you could improve the workplace with what you have just read in this chapter.

SECRET NO.43

- Have regular educational and promotional events on project updates to external customers.

SECRET NO.44

- Develop trained employees so they can competently use the new processes and systems being implemented as a result of a business improvement project such as computer upgrades.

SECRET NO.45

- Have the general manager review the existing business vision/ mission statements and business plans on a regular basis.

∴ The Toolbox

- Pioneers and Innovators

A team must first 'think' in parallel so that its members can begin to 'behave' in a parallel and professional manner.

Anonymous

Night fell. The sounds of creaking crickets and chattering birds slowly subsided as a full moon rose above the horizon to the east of Nirvana.

Muffled coughs and the rustle of blankets could be heard as the four innovation heroes settled in for a good night's sleep. Evening dew started to form on the blades of grass where they slept.

"Steadius, are you still awake?" whispered Associus. "I am now," responded Steadius with dry wit.

"Looking at the stars above, I suddenly realised something. I think we need to give our townsfolk an innovators' toolbox!" said Associus excitedly.

"Ssssshhh, be quiet, go to sleep and talk about it in the morning!" Dominus grunted.

"Associus, move closer towards me and keep the volume down whilst the others rest," instructed Steadius.

Associus did as instructed. "If Nirvana is to maintain its competitive edge, it needs to provide each of the townsfolk with the appropriate set of tools so that they may act as competent and committed leaders of innovation projects," said Associus.

"Associus , doesn't your mind ever stop thinking?" asked Perfectionus wearily as he adjusted the blanket around his neck and shoulders.

Disregarding what Perfectionus had just said, Associus continued. "For our townsfolk to be highly effective, we need to instill confidence in them by being open and transparent with our communications, resolving conflicts successfully, dealing appropriately with the dynamics of newly-formed teams, influencing and motivating others positively, making due delegation and providing good leadership.

"The objective would be for them to be consistent with their actions and behaviour once they have gathered and interpreted the information that we the innovation heroes have provided them."

"Sssssssh, talk about this tomorrow!" repeated an increasingly disgruntled Dominus.

" We should maintain our competence and commitment by keeping our townsfolk informed about the new quest for innovation in Nirvana," pondered Steadius aloud.

"We have to make sure that everyone is thinking and moving in the same direction and yet at the same time develop a sense of personal pride and ownership," added Perfectionus who was now starting to be drawn into this private, late-night conversation.

"Their communication must not be so much in words as in action and conviction. We must provide our future leaders with excellent communication techniques so that they can lift them from their toolboxes when they are required," said Steadius.

"Makes logical sense to me," reinforced Perfectionus.

"I can hear that I am fighting a losing battle," Dominus grumbled as he rolled over to face the silhouettes of Associus and Steadius against the campfire.

"One thing that I have learnt about myself on our journey to Nirvana is that I am not naturally a good listener. I become impatient quickly and want to get on with things," said Dominus.

That Dominus was reflecting upon himself surprised the others. "As strange as this may sound, I have also learnt that the slow way is the fast way," he said profoundly. "If I take the time to listen to people's ideas and contributions, I spend much less time having to follow up with people who aren't doing what I haven't told them," Dominus remarked.

"I wonder if this may have been the cause of many a conflict we used to see you getting involved in," suggested Associus.

"Maybe the greater conflict was not with others but with yourself and you simply did not have the right skills in your innovators' toolbox to manage that effectively," Steadius proffered.

"Well, I hate to admit it but I thrive on challenge, for some unknown reason. Even if one of the townsfolk comes to me with the perfect solution to a problem, I would always argue and debate it," reflected Dominus. I am like a mad dog with a bone, he mused to himself as he scratched his head just behind his left ear like a dog.

"What we all have to realise is that conflict serves a specific purpose here in Nirvana. It is simply a matter of knowing how to deal with it so that it does not turn the townsfolk against each other," commented Perfectionus sagely.

"Although I will naturally avoid conflict, I have found that it is better to resolve it sooner than later. The secret is to harness the energy of the situation by focusing on the issue and not the person," said Associus in his usual diplomatic manner.

"Likewise, I have found that it is important to keep calm during the conflict resolution process and to communicate with logical and factual information," reinforced Steadius.

"Yes, actually, I do find it easy to take the emotion out of the equation," said Perfectionus.

"Then what fun would I have! I get immense joy watching people squirm in my presence," Dominus guffawed.

"They all burst into laughter at Dominus' obviously high level of ignorance on how to resolve conflict appropriately.

"Resolving conflict is simple. First, it is put up or shut up, and then either my way or the highway!" boasted Dominus.

It was a statement that massaged his ego nicely, and he needed it because of his need for power and control. Little did he know that it was really a kink of insecurity in his personal armour that he was trying to hide from others.

"We must realise that conflict is naturally going to occur. It is part of normal human behaviour. Personalities will clash as we move towards becoming a high-performing innovative culture," Associus advised.

"As an innovation hero, the secret is to tap into the frustrations that people are experiencing because it is the people that would have the best possible solutions to drive innovation forward," said Steadius.

"It is all about understanding the dynamics of individuals as they head towards their shared common goal. By doing so, the formal and informal leaders of Nirvana will create unity through diversity," said Associus.

"Talk about verbal diarrhoea," Dominus teased. "The next thing you are going to tell me is that the innovation leader has to be empathetic enough to identify each person's latent ability," scorned Dominus.

"Yes, that is true," said Associus. "Tell me, Dominus, why are you so incongruent with what you say and do? You clearly know what to do, yet, your actions often reveal something quite different."

Dominus remained silent as a stone and his eyes flashed with defiance at Associus' accusations. Not a word was spoken, but a thousand words were sent with one flashing glance of their eyes.

Perfectionus concluded with what he was observing. "The most important action that we can take as innovation heroes is to maintain a high level of team spirit and to provide opportunities to the townsfolk to forge ahead.

"The trick is to develop specific skills that you can place into the innovators' toolbox. Our role as innovation heroes is to get results with and through people. We must have the confidence to motivate and influence the townsfolk of Nirvana to support us on our quest for innovation," stated Perfectionus decisively.

"Here, look at this list that I have been prepared," suggested Associus.

Associus started to read his notes by the light of the full moon and the cloud-free sky.

Checklist - How to influence and motivate others positively

- Recognise and reward good performance.

- Give open, honest and constructive feedback.

- Have a high level of maturity and commitment.

- Be interested in your people by showing them support and giving them encouragement.

- Focus on getting the right person to do the right job.

"Dominus, how would you rate yourself against this checklist?" asked Associus.

Dominus frowned. "Whatever happened to the days when bosses would throw people into the deep end to see if they would sink or swim? Survival of the fittest, that's what I say!"

"That mode of thinking is so far out of date that it is ridiculous. What century are you in, Dominus?" questioned Steadius, not really expecting any answer.

"If it was good enough for me to go through it, then it is good enough for others to go through it as well. Look at me. I turned out perfectly fine," said Dominus.

At that point, the other three innovation heroes turned and looked at one another and burst into laughter.

"Dominus, you will be the first to be issued the innovators' toolbox so that you can quickly develop your competence and commitment. On a serious note, we need to ensure that we are working as a close-knit and professional team. Remember the townsfolk of Nirvana will be looking to us for guidance and direction," said Associus.

"I don't have time to 'wet nurse' anyone," stated Dominus.

"Well, Dominus, you may be in for a surprise," said Perfectionus. "What are you babbling on about?" queried Dominus.

" We need to discuss and then nominate 11 townsfolk from Nirvana to deputise as innovation seekers so that we can groom them to become innovation heroes in the future," said Associus.

"They must be an elite group of individuals that have the capability to overcome adverse situations," said Steadius.

"Perfectionus, could you please pass me everything that we need in order to make our decision on who the 11 innovation seekers of Nirvana would be?" asked Associus politely.

Perfectionus responded immediately with the detailed selection criteria that every innovation seeker must demonstrate in order to reach the shortlist stage of this rigorous process.

"Dominus, I need you to understand that the 11 townsfolk will need to be mentored and we need you to be committed to this initiative," said Steadius.

After giving his word, Dominus exerted his personal power to give the perception that he was in control. He simply stated, "Hurry up then and get on with it. I want to get back to sleep."

"Perfectionus, please could you read out the selection criteria that you have in your file?" Associus requested.

Perfectionus stood alongside the campfire to catch the glow from the steady stream of flowing flames. With notes in hand, he prepared himself and recited that the innovation seekers of Nirvana would have the following skills, knowledge and attributes.

He was rudely interrupted.

"Get on with it, Perfectionus, we don't have all evening!" said Dominus abruptly. "Give me the first sheet of notes. I want to get this show on the road." Holding the list, Dominus read out: "Remember the following when we select and induct the 11 townsfolk from Nirvana who wish to become innovation seekers."

SEED - Thinking

- Strategic and visionary leadership
- Entrepreneurship
- Encouragement of analytical and problem-solving skills
- Decision-making skills

"Here, Associus, it's your turn," said Dominus, taking the neatly laid out papers that were in a logical sequence on the log next to Perfectionus. "Perfectionus is obviously getting caught up in the details of doing the job and not getting on with the job at hand," remarked Dominus.

Associus reached across to receive the second set of notes from Dominus and read out: "Remember the following when we select and induct the 11 Kainotomian townsfolk who wish to become innovation seekers."

GROW - Diversity

- Global mindset
- Respect for opinions
- Open-mindedness
- Wants and values diversity

Associus reflected for a moment before offering Steadius the opportunity to read the next set of selection guidelines for the next group of innovation seekers.

Steadius thought to himself how that made logical sense, and that it was not simply a matter of putting a round peg in a round hole when it came to selecting someone who wanted to be an innovation seeker for Nirvana.

Steadius read: "Remember that there are another five factors that we need to observe of the 11 townsfolk from Nirvana who wish to become innovation pioneers. These are as follows."

SERVE - Talent

- Shares knowledge and information
- Empowers people
- Recruits the right people
- Values life-long learning
- Encourages and supports

Steadius concluded, and commented, "It would make it easy for the selection process if we can use weighted criteria so as to make a sound and solid judgement."

By this stage, Perfectionus was ready. This was because there was only one remaining sheet of paper. He thought to himself: *maybe Dominus was right, maybe I do get caught up too much with the day-to-day details. I can only do my best I suppose.*

"At last! Perfectionus is going to speak!" announced Dominus as Perfectionus moved closer to the light of the campfire to read.

Perfectionus made corrections to his notes as he read. "Remember the following when we select and induct the 11 townsfolk from Nirvana who wish to become innovation seekers.

LEARN - Excellence

- Learns from mistakes
- Eliminates poor performance
- Adopts promising ideas
- Rewards successes and milestones
- Needs to create an innovative environment

"This all makes logical sense to me," said Steadius approvingly. "Perfectionus, there may be one or two items on this list that I may need to emulate," reflected Dominus.

"Only one or two?" mocked Associus.

Perfectionus picked up the personal transcripts of the candidates and asked, "Are we unanimous that these 11 townsfolk from Nirvana fit the criteria for them to become innovation seekers?"

All nodded simultaneously in agreement.

"Good. There is only one more thing to do before we sleep this evening," suggested Dominus. "We must assess that these 11 innovation seekers are appropriate to take our place as innovation heroes in the years to come," suggested Associus.

"Perfectionus, can you please read from the personal transcripts of each candidate how they saw their role as innovation seekers in Nirvana?" instructed Steadius.

On command, Perfectionus quickly recited the following from his well-prepared and documented notes. He was now starting to realise that there was value in being a little impromptu and that not everything had to be a detailed piece of art.

He read with confidence and conviction.

- **Candidate I: Courageus**
  "The innovation seeker needs to be positive and open to new possibilities when exploring new territories. Like our ancient day explorers, he must be confident that there would be treasure in the new territory—are you prepared to go there?"

- **Candidate II: Digitato**
  "An innovation seeker has a fearless soul and is not afraid to experiment with new things. He must have better than 20/20 vision, because he needs to see opportunities where others see a blank."

- **Candidate III: Functionatus**
  "An innovation seeker must be creative and able to influence others on new ideas."

- **Candidate IV: Logisticato**
  "An innovation seeker must have the courage to depart from the norm and have the will to follow his ideas through."

- **Candidate V: Optionedes**
  "An innovation seeker is a person who is organised and logical. He will be a good thinker, team leader and creator who will guide the team to success."

- **Candidate VI: Projectimus**
  "The innovation seeker must be eager to ask both 'why' and 'why not' questions to everything in his environment that is considered conventional. An innovation seeker must be able to put the established vision into practice."

- **Candidate VII: Pragmaticus**
  "An innovation seeker must be able to create new solutions to old problems and have the drive to follow through with these ideas."

- **Candidate VIII: Scenarious**
  An innovation seeker is someone who is not afraid to challenge the present paradigms whether they relate to himself or others. The innovation seeker is a good listener, communicator and thinks outside the box."

- **Candidate IX: Spontaneous**
  "The innovation seeker must always be ready to stimulate fresh and creative ideas. Innovation is a team sport and the seeker must always be willing to play to generate new ideas with new tools."

- **Candidate X: Synchronous**
  "An innovation seeker must be prepared to take risks and withstand the ridicule of his peers and the general public. A good example of this would be our earlier heroes of flight. They were scoffed at, and even regarded as heretics, yet they made it possible for us to fly to destinations all over the world."

"Perfectionus , it amazes me how you have the patience to logically organise this information. Putting the innovation seekers in alphabetical order makes life very easy," acknowledged Associus.

"Okay, everybody, off to sleep, I'm tired," commanded Dominus. The glow of dusk was just beginning to appear as they settled down for the evening. All our innovation heroes began to rest with the excited anticipation of what the next day would bring.

The next day was the day that 11 townsfolk commenced their journey as innovation seekers from Nirvana with dreams of being innovation heroes respected by all.

Dominus proclaimed before he slept. "My friends, I look forward to developing the innovation seekers on this quest for innovation in Nirvana."

With that, the other three innovation heroes slept peacefully knowing that Dominus fully supported the development of leaders and teams to champion innovation in Nirvana.

Go to the Innovation Hit List at the back of this book and consider how you could improve the workplace with what you have just read in this chapter.

SECRET NO.46

- Have the heads of departments develop area business plans with key performance indicators in consultation with frontline managers.

SECRET NO.47

- Have the organisation's frontline managers implement and monitor projects and initiatives in consultation with team players.

SECRET NO.48

- Have all team players be accountable and responsible for tasks that were delegated to them.

⁖Corporate Theatre

- The Journey's Script

> *The process of succeeding can be seen as a series of trials in which your vision constantly guides you toward your target while in your actual performance you are regularly slightly off target. Success in any area requires constantly readjusting your behaviour as the result of feedback from your experience.*
>
> **Michael Gelb and Tony Buzan**

Congratulations! You are now well on your way to mastering innovation!

As a hero, the journey now begins for you. By completing this book, it automatically demonstrates that you are serious about creating an innovative environment. You have also shown that you are someone who has the commitment and drive to follow through on any action that you take.

I have created this Corporate Theatre script to assist you in transferring your learning back to the workplace. Engage your team to support you on your quest.

This script has been written with masculine forms for ease and simplicity. Switch the characters to the feminine, if you wish. The magical land of Corporate Utopia is called Nirvana — it means a transcendent state in which there is neither suffering, desire, nor sense of self, and our towns people can be released from the effects of karma and the corporate life cycle of death and rebirth. But remember my friends – there are no short cuts in Nirvana. It represents our final goal!

Have fun with this. You can make this as elaborate or as simple as you wish. We recommend that you request that people become creative with their production. This will assist you in developing a dynamic and innovative working environment.

Get a team of five people together and allocate them specific roles. To maximise the learning, apply a natural 'best fit' role methodology between the people you choose and the characters they are to play. Look for people who naturally demonstrate the various behavioural traits within the workplace.

Apart from the Narrator, you will also need four other volunteers to take on the roles of Dominus, Associus, Steadius and Perfectionus.

Character Roles

Brief descriptions of the characters—their natural traits and evil spirits, are given below. This will assist your acting team to get into the role of the assigned character.

Characters	Natural Traits	Evil Spirits
Dominus	Power, control, status, ego, quick results, challenge	Failure, Loss of control, Being taken advantage of
Associus	Harmony, recognition, being liked and accepted, prestige	Rejection, Isolation
Steadius	Appreciation, logical processes, routine, security, loyalty, systems	Insecurity, Change
Perfectionus	Details, specifications, standards, guarantees, proven methods	Chaos, Criticism of performance

⸬The Script

Narrator	The four characters, Dominus, Associus, Steadius and Perfectionus, were now sitting by the warm campfire as the sun began to set on yet another interesting and challenging day.
	After a period of time, their discussions turned into personal reflection on how they could control their 'evil spirits of inner conflict' whilst they go in search of the magic land of Corporate Utopia and the town known as Nirvana. Unusual as it was for Dominus, he managed to take the time to sit down and reflect. After thirty minutes of introspective thinking, he mustered the courage to share his feelings and findings with the other innovation heroes.
Dominus (assertive and abrupt manner)	Well, let me tell you about myself. I have come to the realisation that I am a person who is often direct and forceful. I have a drive to achieve, wherever possible, the perfect solution.
	I am a self-starter who enjoys a variety of tasks, be they challenging or demanding. I also prefer to work alone. I dislike being reliant upon teams and other people because they slow me down.

Despite my somewhat overly assertive approach, I am internally reflective and have an innate need to explore new and interesting situations, as long as I can see opportunity within a situation for me.

I am exceedingly active and will show urgency in most situations. Because of this, I may bypass convention by being very strong-willed.

Providing that things are going well and my way, I can also be forward looking.

Narrator	By this stage, the other three characters were in awe of Dominus' honesty. They all thought: this is a first.
Associus (supportive and friendly voice)	Dominus, I would like to hear what else you have learnt about yourself on this journey to Nirvana.
Dominus (strong, assertive and confident voice)	Well, I assume responsibility in all dealings because I am goal-minded and a very strong decision-maker. There may be times where I am seen as too demanding, impatient and inflexible by others.

	There are also indications that I may be lacking in both sympathy and empathy. People have told me that I sometimes intimidate them. I simply think they are weak. Whilst paperwork and administration details are not my strongest points, you can be assured that if a result depends upon getting the facts and figures, then I will force myself to do just that.
Perfectionus (incredulous and surprised voice)	Tell us more, Dominus.
Dominus (assertive and impatient voice)	Well, I am motivated by independence of both the rules and people. I also need room to move and authority to act without constraint. I also need to have my authority accepted. It is my way or the highway. I have a continual need to win and to prove my ability, and to be recognised as an achiever in my formal or informal positions in the workplace.
Associus (friendly and sincere voice)	Dominus, that is an interesting insight into yourself. Would you like to hear a few words of how I would describe you?

Dominus (confident but hesitant voice/ takes adeep breath in preparation for feedback)	Go ahead, Associus. You have caught me in a good mood!
Associus (friendly and sincere voice)	I would describe you by the following words: driven, demanding, self-starting, forceful, independent, opinionated, blunt, strong-willed, restless, anxious, active, energetic, probing, skeptical and you continually ask 'what' and'when' questions.
Dominus (assertive and relieved voice)	Thank you, Associus. Maybe this is where my 'evil spirits of inner conflict' come from.
Steadius (logical and non-emotional voice)	Possibly. But in what way, Dominus?
Narrator	Dominus went on to explain that his 'evil spirits of inner conflict' were now becoming clearer and got the better of him from time to time.

Dominus (strong and reflective voice)	The evil spirits of inner conflict are now becoming clear and often get the better of me from time to time. I have a natural fear of failure, being taken advantage of and losing control of my environment. I now understand that my personal development opportunities will be to:

- Learn to pace myself better and know when and how to relax.
- Become aware of the type of needs that other people have—as well as my own needs.
- Have an understanding that everyone needs social contact and relationship supp ort at times.
- Accept the importance of existing rules and policies as part of the process of getting things done.

Perfectionus (non-emotional and friendly voice)	Excellent work!

Dominus (assertive and challenging voice)	Now that I have told you about myself, it is time that you tell me about yourself, Associus.

Associus (excited and friendly voice)	Well, friends, this is what I have discovered about myself since I began this journey to Nirvana.
Narrator	Associus went on to proclaim the following about himself.
Associus (excited and friendly voice)	I am an outgoing and independent person who enjoys varying environments and situations.
	I am socially competitive, verbally persuasive and rather charming. I have the ability to put across and sell my own ideas and others' ideas, products and concepts, optimistically and enthusiastically.
	I realise that I am sometimes very pushy because of my enthusiasm although I am not by nature aggressive or antagonistic to others.
	My need is to inspire others, but I could be perceived as being too fast-paced for some people, especially Perfectionus. I certainly enjoy popularity and being in the limelight. I will seek opportunities to obtain public recognition from my peers.

	I have found that I am not naturally decisive and particularly dislike making harsh decisions as this may make me unpopular. I also dislike repetitive work and I am often inattentive to detail. Although I am a good starter at projects, I tend to leave the finishing and servicing to others.
Dominus (blunt and abrupt voice)	How true is that!
Associus (excited and friendly voice)	I may come across as being more assertive than what I really am. This is probably due to my high degree of verbal independence. I have a high degree of work energy. I am quick paced, mobile, alert and variety orientated. I am also good at painting the big picture and creating optimism and enthusiasm in others.
Steadius (non-emotional and encouraging voice)	Tell us more.

Associus (excited and proud/ friendly voice)	Okay, I do not mind at all, because I love being the centre of attention. I am motivated by popularity, independence, variety, change and having money for the good life. I also enjoy being generous and will seek opportunities to promote my ideas and myself.
Steadius (non-emotional and supportive friendly voice)	Associus, that is an interesting insight into yourself. Would you like to hear a few words of how I would describe you?
Narrator	Sitting down calmly on the cool rock in preparation for the feedback, Associus thought to himself: I hope they still like me after what I have just said about myself.
Steadius (non-emotional and supportive friendly voice)	I would describe you as being independent, self-willed, verbal, active, optimistic, enthusiastic, self-promoting, friendly, outgoing, sociable, communicative, quick starter, mild, non-aggressive and someone who asks 'who' questions frequently.
Narrator	Associus went on to explain that his 'evil spirits of inner conflict' were also becoming clearer.

Associus (optimistic and reflective friendly voice)	The 'evil spirit s of inner conflict' are now becoming clearer to me. I now realise that I have a natural fear of rejection, isolation and being ostracised by people at work. I now understand that my personal development opportunities will be to:

- Learn to develop more organised & systematic approaches to doing things. This includes following through with proven work methods.
- Be more realistic with expectations and objectives when working in a team and not to be overly optimistic.
- Understand how and when to be firm and direct in dealing with less favourable situations— especially with Dominus.
- Accept the importance of completing work tasks and agreements with people according to priority commitments agreed with them.

Steadius (non-emotional and supportive voice)	Excellent work.

Associus (friendly and encouraging voice)	Now that I have told you about myself, the floor is yours. It is now time that you tell us about your learning, Steadius.
Narrator	Steadius stepped up to the light of the fire with some reluctance.
Steadius (non-emotional and reluctant voice)	I would see myself as a steady and reliable individual with a great deal of patience and quiet tenacity. I am independent with both people and the rules and rarely antagonise others deliberately. I realise that I am very stubborn and could well challenge the establishment if I feel that an injustice has occurred. It is important to realise that I am justice-oriented as opposed to rule-oriented. Because of this, I am a hard worker who likes to get on with the job by taking a practical approach at my own pace. I find that if others try to hurry me along, my reaction is likely to be one of quiet, but dogged defiance. Sometimes, I am self-conscious and some people may misinterpret my non-demonstrativeness as aloofness, but I am not aloof. In fact, I am usually team-oriented.

I have now come to the realisation that I am a good anchor and administrator for any team that I am a part of because I have the ability to cope with both routine and repetitive work, albeit not at a low level because I like to use my brains.

I do not need a great deal of guidance but I do require a clear understanding of the tasks to be undertaken. I now understand that I have a tendency to avoid decision-making, particularly quick decisions, as well as those that are harsh and/or unpopular. I also do not enjoy disciplining others

As a deep thinker, I very often have good ideas. However, there is a tendency for me to keep these ideas to myself unless asked.

Dominus (challenging and friendly voice)	Steadius, I must commend you on your logic and rationale of your learning whilst being in search of innovation. What else can you tell us?
Narrator	Steadius went on to say that he sought sincere appreciation for a job well done and needed security of employment via a job contract. He also commented that he liked having the time to assess situations before acting on them.
	He also valued the written form of feedback.
	He discovered that he was wary of insincere praise and would seek genuineness from his peers and superiors.

Steadius (non-emotional and questioning voice)	Perfectionus, I would like to know which words best describe me.
Narrator	Perfectionus gathered his thoughts to deliver the following message precisely.
Perfectionus (matter-of-fact voice)	I would describe you as being kind, self-conscious, thorough, patient, independent, hardworking, loyal, sincere, indirect, non-demanding, dependable, mild, unassuming, stubborn, tenacious, administrative, practical, and persistent. You frequently ask 'how' questions
Narrator	Steadius went on to summarise that his 'evil spirits of inner conflict' are change and insecurity.

Steadius (non-emotional and reflective voice)	My 'evil spirits of inner conflict' are change and insecurity. I now understand that my personal development opportunities will be to: • Learn how to better handle the reality of unexpected and ongoing change. • Be aware of when to delegate to other people to achieve desired results. • Have an understanding of how to be more assertive with people when taking charge of situations. • Develop and accept the opportunity to grow by learning to do new and different things in a variety of ways other than my own standard approaches.
Perfectionus (matter-of-fact voice)	Again, sound and solid findings with a good structure and conclusion, my friend
Dominus (assertive and challenging voice)	What about you, Perfectionus? Are you prepared to share with us your findings about yourself whilst on this journey to Nirvana?
Perfectionus (nervous and hesitant voice)	I will do my best.

Associus (humorous and friendly voice)	As you always do. Would you have it any other way?
Narrator	Perfectionus stood tall, adjusted his clothes and glasses, and then proceeded to unravel the neatly-folded notes that he had written throughout the quest. Perfectionus read:
Perfectionus (matter-of-fact and non-emotional voice)	I see myself as a systematic and precise thinker and worker who tends to follow procedures in my personal and business lives. I tend to proceed in an orderly and predetermined manner. I rarely antagonise people consciously and normally act in a highly tactful and diplomatic fashion. I must say, however, that I have sometimes caught myself being passive-aggressive by not participating and following through on things. Most of the time, I demonstrate a good sense of timing and shrewdness in selecting the right decision at the right time. Being an extremely conscientious person, I am able to do painstaking work that requires accuracy and maintaining standards. Some people accuse me of being anal-retentive. I like to think of it as being thorough.

I enjoy standard operating procedures —no sudden or abrupt departures from the standards. Change is okay only when I have had time to think through all of the implications of the change.

I prefer to share responsibilities in areas where I do not have total knowledge or expertise, and may at times look for reassurance from others. This is because I don't like being criticised.

I do not like spending excessive time away from my home and family. I need work assignments that are precisely planned. I may need support from others when dealing with unfamiliar and unknown tasks that require high levels of expertise, knowledge or technical know-how.

Detailed explanations are essential at times of change to ensure that I have the full knowledge, understanding and logical rationale behind the changes. If I don't get this information, then I just won't move.

Due to my very own high standards, I much prefer to work with fellow specialists and experts rather than generalists. I may be seen as very systematic, precise and proficient, and I demand a similar attitude from co-workers and team members.

Associus simply annoys me because I think that he lacks depth and substance.

Associus	Perfectionus, you amaze me with your ability to turn human behaviour into a logical science. Well done! Is there anything else you would like to share with us?
(excited and proud friendly voice)	

Narrator	Perfectionus went on to recite the following from his well-documented notes.

Perfectionus	Yes, Associus.
(matter-of-fact and non-emotional voice)	I am a person who is motivated by clarity in work expectations, the security of the situation and the status quo. I normally need to feel accepted by the organisation but not necessarily to be a part of it.
	Reputation, accuracy and preciseness are very important to me. You may often find me seeking opportunities to work alone or on the periphery of a team because I need to have access to details, instructions and guidelines for reference—not people.

Dominus	Are you ready for some feedback?
(assertive and challenging voice)	

Perfectionus (matter-of-fact and non-emotional voice)	Only if it is specific, factual and logical.
Dominus (assertive and reflective voice)	Okay, I will be stretching my natural behaviour on this one, but I will give it a go.
	I see you as accurate, precise, detailed, skeptical, probing, systematic, logical, deliberate, analytical, wary, self-conscious, reflective, non-aggressive, and asks 'why' and someone who asks 'when' questions frequently.
Perfectionus (matter-of-fact and non-emotional voice)	Thank you, Dominus. Your feedback provides me with clarity to what my natural fears are—insecurity and criticism of performance.
Narrator	Perfectionus continued reciting his findings from the neatly scripted notes.

Perfectionus (matter-of-fact and non-emotional voice)	I have learnt the following about controlling my' evil spirits of inner conflict': • To learn to develop a greater tolerance for conflict and human imperfection, including developing realistic approaches to prevent and minimise conflict between people. • To be aware of the importance of more direct communication and to discuss my views with others. • To develop an understanding of different types of talents and interest levels of individuals when trying to achieve desired objectives. • To accept that I am a worthwhile person in my own right, and not only for what I do.
Associus (friendly and caring voice)	Let us reflect for a moment so that we can learn from our past experiences and current lessons which will help us in the future.
Steadius (non-emotional and friendly voice)	That's right. By giving and receiving open and honest feedback about what we know about ourselves and about what others know about us, we have the ability to remain open because we've reduced any blind spots and eliminated false impressions that we may have of our own personalities and abilities.
Dominus (loud and abrupt voice)	Sounds like a waste of time to me.

Narrator	On that comment, they all turned to one another with stunned looks of surprise.
Dominus	I think...we should start today.
(humble voice)	Checking the results – Five powerful questions

> ● Can you relate any of the characters in this corporate theatre with people in your workplace?
> ● In this corporate theatre, which character best reflects you?
> ● Which characters are the easiest and hardest to get along with?
> ● Which character reflects your current boss and what makes him/ her easy or hard to get on with?
> ● Why is it important to embrace workplace diversity when creating an innovative working environment?

⫶Self-Assessment

- Change and Innovation Survey

Take 15 minutes to complete the following survey. You will immediately identify the critical factors that will help your High Potential Leaders develop strategies to gain commitment and support for innovation.

Evaluate each criterion in terms of how you would rate the current demonstrated levels of performance. The criteria can be seen on the next page.

- 1 = Very Low level of demonstrated performance

- 2 = Low level of demonstrated performance

- 3 = Moderate level of demonstrated performance

- 4 = High level of demonstrated performance

- 5 = Very High level of demonstrated performance

Reflect on the behaviours and actions that you have observed in the workplace in the past three months. You can focus on the entire organisation or you can focus on your department.

As a High Potential Leader, these are the first steps to take as you go on your quest for change and innovation.

	Criteria	Current level of performance				
	Do you have....	Very Low				Very High
1	...commitment from all employees for developing an innovative working environment?	1	2	3	4	5
2	...innovative initiatives linked to Key Performance Indicators?	1	2	3	4	5
3	...a clear purpose and objective when creating an innovative working environment?	1	2	3	4	5
4	...identified timeframes and deadlines when undertaking initiatives or projects?	1	2	3	4	5
5	...an identified 'hit list' of ideas that focuses people on continuous improvement opportunities?	1	2	3	4	5
6	...identified roles and responsibilities when undertaking initiatives and projects in the workplace?	1	2	3	4	5
7	...a proactive process of building commitment towards allocated projects and initiatives?	1	2	3	4	5

	Criteria	Current level of performance				
	Do you have....	Very Low				Very High
8	...a strategy to maintain the organisation's innovative and competitive edge?	1	2	3	4	5
9	...people proactively investigating opportunities that will lead to improvements in effectiveness and efficiencies within the workplace?	1	2	3	4	5
10	...a structured communication process that enhances open communication throughout the workplace?	1	2	3	4	5
11	...a positive working environment with minimum conflict between workgroups?	1	2	3	4	5
12	...a decision-making process that reinforces fairness and equity?	1	2	3	4	5
13	...a structured and standardised process for decision-making?	1	2	3	4	5
14	...flexibility in adapting to change that is caused from external or internal influences?	1	2	3	4	5
15	...initiatives and projects that positively support cost-effectiveness and efficiency strategies?	1	2	3	4	5

	Criteria	Current level of performance				
	Do you have....	Very Low				Very High
16	...interesting and challenging job functions because of workplace initiatives and projects?	1	2	3	4	5
17	...a structured process which ensures that the correct innovation initiative is selected?	1	2	3	4	5
18	...shared ownership between employees and managers that supports initiatives or projects?	1	2	3	4	5
19	...effective management practices that ensure all initiatives and projects will have a positive impact in the workplace?	1	2	3	4	5
20	...feedback from internal or external customers to clearly identify their needs when undertaking workplace projects and initiatives?	1	2	3	4	5
21	...a communication strategy to reduce 'fear of change' in individuals and teams when going through change?	1	2	3	4	5
22	...effective communication processes to reduce the levels of frustration of individuals and teams?	1	2	3	4	5

	Criteria	Current level of performance				
	Do you have....	**Very Low**				**Very High**
23	...financial rewards and incentives to reinforce positive workplace behaviour?	1	2	3	4	5
24	...a number of 'quick wins on the board' when undertaking new projects and initiatives?	1	2	3	4	5
25	...people encouraging innovative thinking that supports the organisational goals and objectives?	1	2	3	4	5
26	...active involvement from employees and management to get 'buy in and support' for initiatives and projects?	1	2	3	4	5
27	...initiatives and projects as a means to capture, ignite and utilise the corporate intelligence?	1	2	3	4	5
28	...department leaders at all levels who 'walk the talk' and act as positive role models?	1	2	3	4	5
29	...an immediate leader who 'walks the talk' and acts as a positive role model?	1	2	3	4	5
30	...input from the team to develop commitment, accountability and responsibility?	1	2	3	4	5

	Criteria	Current level of performance				
	Do you have....	**Very Low**				**Very High**
31	...department leaders who reinforce and communicate the need and benefits of being innovative and competitivein the marketplace?	1	2	3	4	5
32	...the time and space that allow for the thinking of alternative approaches?	1	2	3	4	5
33	...opportunities to gain government funding that supports your current innovation initiatives and projects?	1	2	3	4	5
34	...initiatives and projects that are easily measured with clearly defined outcomes?	1	2	3	4	5
35	...a strategic plan with clear goals, objectives and key performance indicators?	1	2	3	4	5
36	...a breakdown of tasks and milestones with clear timelines when undertaking projectsand initiatives?	1	2	3	4	5
37	... informal reward and recognition processes for individuals?	1	2	3	4	5
38	... formal reward and recognition processes for individuals, such as performance appraisals?	1	2	3	4	5

	Criteria	Current level of performance				
	Do you have....	Very Low				Very High
39	...regular celebrations to reinforce, reward and sell the benefits and outcomes of projects and initiative successes?	1	2	3	4	5
40	...clear job roles and descriptions with identified accountabilities?	1	2	3	4	5
41	...regular educational and promotional events on project updates for internal customers?	1	2	3	4	5
42	...regular educational and promotional events on project updates for external customers?	1	2	3	4	5
43	...trained employees who can competently use the new processes and systems being implemented as a result of a business improvement project, such as computer upgrades?	1	2	3	4	5
44	...a general manager who reviews the existing business vision/ mission statements and business plans on a regular basis?	1	2	3	4	5
45	...heads of departments who develop area business plans with KPIs in consultation with frontline managers?	1	2	3	4	5

	Criteria	Current level of performance				
	Do you have....	Very Low				Very High
46	...frontline managers who · implement and monitor projects and initiatives in consultation with team players?	1	2	3	4	5
47	...team players who are accountable and action-oriented with projects and initiatives that have been delegated to them?	1	2	3	4	5

Top8	Criteria(Insert Criterion Number and/or Description)	Rate the level of priority		
		Low	Medium	High
1				
2				
3				
4				
5				
6				
7				
8				

Words of Wisdom

A single step will not create a dance, so a single thought will not make a pattern in your mind. To make a beautiful dance you learn to step again and again. To make a deep mental pattern you must think over and over the kind of thoughts you wish to dominate your life.

Erica Anderton
Australia
∾o∾

Fundamentally, all people are lazy.
So you need to put in place fool proof systems to compensate for this.

Anonymous
∾o∾

Eighty percent of success is simply showing up and making a commitment.

Anonymous
∾o∾

A manager may think he knows what is going on in the workplace. But, it is actually the workers who do.

Anonymous

❧

Always listen to your frontline staff.
The most practical and workable ideas usually come from those at the coalface!

Stephen Baker
Australia

❧

If you are looking for recognition and plaudits for being a leader, you are not being the best leader you can be.

Paul Barton
Australia

❧

Never let success at work be to the detriment of your health.

David Beard
Australia

❧

When my cupboard is bare, both physically and mentally
My resolve is retail therapy for both!
(hahahaha)

***

I truly believe in the work of angels

Leanne Bedford
Australia
∾o∾

Character is Destiny.

Andrew Bloom
Australia
∾o∾

Imagination rules the world.

Napoleon Bonaparte
the 'Emperor of the French'
∾o∾

Honesty is about adherence and Integrity is about conduct.
Be exactly who you say you are, scare the world.

John Bostock
Australia
∾o∾

<u>On the topic of Leadership</u>
People follow people they have a reason to trust.
What reason do they have to trust you?

<u>On the topic of Change</u>
I disagree people are hard wired to resist change. Most people deal with much bigger changes in their personal lives than changes organisations require of them.

It is up to us to develop the strategy and provide the leadership that will help them hopefully embrace, and at least deal with, our organisational change.

Gordon Brockway
Australia

ﾐﾟｏﾐﾟ

My personal philosophy is that not only am I responsible for my own life, but by doing the best in this moment ensures I'm in the best place for the next moment.

This philosophy is my driving force and helps me guide others to be accountable and maintain an accountable culture within the business!

Allison Cairns

Australia

ﾐﾟｏﾐﾟ

As a workplace leader, never lose being a down-to-earth person - you will go arse up!

Mario Camer-Pesci
Australia

❧

Success is happiness.

Mary Camer-Pesci
Australia

❧

Sometimes sitting around and waiting is the best way forward.

Wendy Campbell
Australia

❧

Method is much, technique is much, but inspiration is even more.

Benjamin Nathan Cardozo
the late American jurist

❧

It is not whether you win or lose -
it is how you play the game!

**Written by Grantland Rice and
submitted by Choi Yong-Min**
Korea

∽o∼

When unhappy with a team's performance, it often helps to
communicate or re-iterate what your expectations are.

It may be the first time it has been articulated to the team!

Nic Christodoulou
Australia

∽o∼

Our greatest glory, is not in never failing but in rising up
anytime we fail. Little minds have little worries, but big minds
have no time for worries.

**Written by Ralph Waldo Emerson and
submitted by Chua Heng Chin**
Singapore

∽o∼

We must beware of needless innovations,
especially when guided by logic.

Winston Churchill
the late British prime minister

∽o∼

People who take risks are the happiest and most successful.
You can't live your dreams without taking a risk.

Tracey Cleeman
Australia
∞

Words about surviving:
Courage is the primary virtue.
Be true to yourself above all else.
Major on the Majors and Minor on the minors.
If it can be fixed with money is it a real issue

My get over yourself statement:
In 500 years who will remember my name?

Christopher Colyer
Australia
∞

Achieving your goals is hard work
Quitting your goals is harder.

Mike Daggett
America
∞

Don't lose focus of your end goal. Sometimes the journey takes longer than you planned but if you keep moving forward you will get there.

The universe is conspiring to make it happen; it didn't say it would make it easy. But it will make it happen!

Kylie Dalton
Australia
∾o∾

It's not what you don't know, it's what you know that you don't realise that you know. Lack of effort causes failure - NOT lack of ability. When the negative little voice in your head rambles on stop talking to it!

If you shoot for the moon and miss you still end up amongst the stars.

Alan Davis
Australia
∾o∾

What we anticipate seldom occurs;
what we least expect generally happens.

Benjamin Disraeli
the late British prime minister
∾o∾

Most people want to do a great job;
awesome leaders create places where they can.

David Evenis
Australia
ᘒᘒ

It takes a Klingon's viewpoint to understand Aussie culture!

Jeff Garbutt
Australia
ᘒᘒ

Informed leaders lead by precise example!

Bob Glasheen
Australia
ᘒᘒ

Finding utopia and maintaining harmony in any work setting, really, (corporate, NFP, government) is about developing an internal strength around core morals / fundamentals.

This will be strengthened and shaped by surrounding yourself with people who respect those core morals / fundamentals and operate in a similar manner. The harmony then needs to be balanced by the ability to extend outside of your comfort zone.

This 'stretch' can be a personal one or within the work setting to achieve something greater than what could be done alone. The metamorphosis and journey is the real beauty.

Lacy Gow
Australia
∾o∾

Lift your head up and see the world.

Engage with all its people, you never know where your next inspiration will come from.

Kerran Hobbs
Australia
∾o∾

Given the constant winds of workplace change - best be like a tumbleweed – and just keep rolling!

Leisa Irving
Australia
∾o∾

Sometimes when you innovate, you make mistakes. It is best to admit them quickly, and get on with improving your other innovations.

Steve Jobs
co-founder of Apple computers
෴

To achieve true enlightenment one must move through life with eyes open wide.

Be willing to experience the lows as easily as the highs. This is what gives one the strength and the knowledge to become not just a good leader BUT a great leader.

Deb Jones
Australia
෴

Mindless habitual behaviour
is the enemy of innovation.

Rosabeth Moss Kanter
American business speaker and consultant
෴

Let us never negotiate out of fear.
But let us never fear to negotiate.

John Fitzgerald Kennedy
the late American president

∞

The harder I try the luckier I get!

Colin Kerr
Australia

∞

Don't put off till tomorrow, what you can do today!

Dot and Tom Kinnaird
Australia

∞

Always remember to have a twerk-life balance.

Lance Kinnaird
Australia

∞

When making a tough decision, for example a high potential leader has a moment of indiscretion, err on the side of safety. Don't ignore the safety incident or hope it will resolve itself. Whatever your decision, check it against your conscience.

If you think it's too harsh to let someone go, consider having to tell a grieving spouse and mother of three that her husband won't be returning home at the end of a shift because someone else deserved a second chance.

Wendy Leukuma
America

ထာ၀ာ

Building TRUST – in Leadership
Total service leadership in all that they do.
Rewarding integrity, honesty and respect from within their organisation.
Understanding & empathising with their organisation's needs.
Setting the standards for ethical behavior.
Through teamwork & innovation.

Rob Lewis
Australia

ထာ၀ာ

Do not let inertia become the root cause of your failures!

I think that the greatest enemy to innovation in any organization is the failure to act quickly enough on potentially great ideas evolved from discussions by many people who invested precious amount time thinking them out.

One of the reasons for this non-action could be the lingering fear in the leaders'/ team members' minds
that the ideas would fail.

Gilbert Loh
Singapore
∽o∾

People begin to become successful
the minute they decide to be.

Harvey Mackay
bestselling author of
**Swim with the Sharks
(Without Being Eaten Alive)**
∽o∾

Always remain true to your core values and every personal or business decision will be that much easier.

Greg MacKenzie
Australia
∽o∾

Every day you delay your marketing
is a gift to your competition.

Sherryn McBride
Australia
ᑲᲿᑐ

Inspiring staff to perform at their best is something that is intrinsic within the art of team and personal communication. Staff respond to the behaviour of respect and when being listened to positively, they will respond by giving their best with excellent ideas and increased productivity.

This adds real value at all opportunities when they are feeling that they are part of the business team.

Peter McKenzie
Australia
ᑲᲿᑐ

The basics of learning is "basics"
to win, stick with the rules of basics.

Teams win deals, challenge a team and they will deliver.

As a leader if you try on your own, you will be slow and competition will beat you. Use your winning team and make them proud.

Struggle on in spite of adverse conditions. You have it within you to triumph in whatever you choose to do. A goal attained, a duty done or a task completed - the reward should be worthwhile, and the glow of pride the best sensation.

Baravand Madhav
South Africa
∽o∾

As leaders we should observe more and allow team members to be part of the decision making process more often.

Derick Mitchell
South Africa
∽o∾

Learn all - question all.

Frédéric Moraillon
Singapore
∽o∾

The 3 E's of successful business
Engage - With all stakeholders, including customers, staff and communities.
Enhance - Drive efficiency, improve quality, performance and the customer experience.
Evolve - Change and adapt to your environment.

Craig Moulton
Australia
∽o∾

Don't be afraid to seek advice.
Someone, somewhere at some time
has already been through this.

Mark Newman
Australia
∽o∾

You will always miss 100% of the shots you don't take!

In other words you can't succeed unless you give it a go, that means you have to take action. Seek and You Shall Find!

Every problem or situation has a solution you just need to find the right solution and/or the best solution for that situation.

Santa Nicotra
Australia
∽o∾

Leaders, build confidence in your workmates,
back them to succeed and team members ask workmates,
how should I help you?

Evan Nunn
Australia
∾○∾

When coming into a new organisation, always do your history
and geography lessons before making changes. To get to your
next job, do yourself out of your current job.

What you leave out is just as important as what you leave in.

My own experience:

Wisdom is intelligence with heart.
Define yourself through your relationships with
others and yourself.
True leadership greatness is when you are prepared to
promote good talent above yourself.
Pay it forward and make a difference, no matter how small.
No one is indispensable but everyone brings their unique
qualities.

Natalie Ong
Australia
∾○∾

The secret to happiness is to reverse the fundamental economic problem of unlimited wants and limited resources. If you limit your wants, you'll find plenty of resources.

Paul Owen
Australia
༨༠༡

Exhibit your passion - Share your vision - Lead with purpose!

Pat Persico
America
༨༠༡

Get it right, the first time, every time!

This comes from experience in that we never seem to have enough time to do things properly in the first place, yet we somehow manage to find stacks of time later on to fix the problems from rushing things.

If we spent a bit more time up front and focused on getting it right the first time, all that time previously spent fixing up problems could be used for more value adding activities.

Ron Philippkowski
Australia
༨༠༡

The chief enemy of creativity is 'good' sense.

Pablo Picasso
the late Spanish artist and painter

≈o≈

No matter the problem - it comes down to CRAP!
Competency
Resources
Attitude
Processes

David Richards
Australia

≈o≈

Everyday I set goals and break tasks down into
smaller portions.

I can't be all things to all people,
so I have to be true to myself and the people closest to me.

Shelley Richards
Australia

≈o≈

Know your own brand and always work on it!

Maria Saraceni
Australia

≈o≈

Leadership is leading from the front and not following.
There is no "I" in the word team.
As a leader one needs to Communicate,
Listen and Communicate.
Good leaders can make decisions.

Roy Sargeant
Australia
ᥫ᭡ꙮᥫ᭡

If there is a will, there is a way.
Cut the red tape where needed to achieve the goals and stand
firm to take the responsibility as a leader.

Organisations need more people to challenge, think out of the
box and take the responsibility in order to advance and
excel in its trade!

Matti Siitonen
Singapore
ᥫ᭡ꙮᥫ᭡

Kids are more perceptive than adults!!!
Politics and ego are less likely to get in the way and
edit what they say!
Get out there, get talking and get listening to people.
And importantly, get back to them – ALWAYS!

Dani Sirotic
Australia
ᥫ᭡ꙮᥫ᭡

Feel free to over achieve!

Lorene Smithers
Australia

∞⊙∞

On the topic of ethics in business and management:
The right thing isn't always the easy thing
but it's always the right thing.

On the topic of leadership
and the pace of today's business world:

In today's fast-moving world
the notion of leadership has changed.

Plan? Of course! But if you are brave enough to employ the
right people you must also be prepared to point to the beacon
on the hill and then hold on for the ride!

Marcus Stafford
Australia

∞⊙∞

Becoming rich has more to do with how much you spend and
what you spend it on, than how much you earn.
Business is full of risks, just make sure you calculate them and
take the ones that are in your favour.

Fabio Suffell
Australia

∞⊙∞

Trust is an asset that is slow to build but it can be quick to lose. Leaders should never underestimate the impact of their actions on the trust of their followers.

Lea Symonds
Australia
∽o∽

The greatest tragedy is not failing
but succeeding in things that don't matter finally!

Daniell Tam
Singapore
∽o∽

You cannot buy Respect and Trust.
These are bestowed upon great leaders.

Karen Tay
Singapore
∽o∽

In today's turbulent and complex business world, in trying to differentiate your business value proposition,
I found it's not enough to be the best at what you do, but instead - to be the only one who does what you do.
The ultimate strategic advantage,
the Nirvana of strategic advantage!

Dominique Thatcher
Australia
∽o∽

Don't allow things to become a problem that cloud your mind into negativity, but rather a challenge that excites to be overcome and defeated.

Craig Thomas
Australia
∽०∾

When negotiating difficult issues.
Always try to see the issue or
situation from the other person's perspective.
This helps to achieve an acceptable solution.

John Venables
Australia
∽०∾

Focus: Company and Customer Focus

I have seen, regretfully, a shift in the 'Focus' of companies, away from the customer, to the bottom line.

Ultimately, the short-term gains (cost cutting etc) are lost against the customer movement away, in search of better 'Customer Service'. The bottom line is created from the customer. The successful companies have maintained their 'Focus' on the Customer.

I often describe this to people by saying when you physically serve a customer; you look them in the 'eye' and assist them. Imagine looking at someone's shoes (the bottom line) and saying - can I help you?

It simply does not work and sadly,
a lot of companies don't even know they are doing it.

Michael Wake
Australia

∽o∽

Never give up; Work as a team;
Don't have one look and say it's too hard!

Louis Oliver Walkden
Australia

∽o∽

Successful leadership is about being the 'ringmaster' who
is very aware of what people can bring to the success of the
business, or in other words, understanding how to apply
*'human capital - talents, knowledge, skills, experience, creativity,
resourcefulness and attitude'.*

What makes a great leader is how they best utilise these
human elements to achieve the best for both business success,
and for their people to feel part of and satisfied with their part
of that success.

Anna Ward
Australia

∽o∽

Resist temptation to give the answers;
just keep asking great questions.

Align what you say, think and do
and you won't trip yourself up down the line.

Authentic and immediate feedback
should not be an opportunity lost.

Natalie Whiteside
Australia
∽૦∾

Time is not a commodity for us to "save" it is actually a
currency for us to "spend" and for us the value is in the wise
spending not the thrifty saving.

Spend time doing the things that bring you
joy and value the time you have.

It does not last forever - spend wisely.

Steven Wren
Australia
∽૦∾

Once you adopt the Positive Thinking Approach,
you are on your way to Success!

On the contrary, if you adopt the Negative Thinking Approach,
you are taking few steps backwards from your Goal of Success!

Think Positive Always!

Richard Young
Singapore
ﾍﾟﾟ0ﾟﾟ

Believe in your skills - you have earned them.
Believe that they are transferable and they will be.

Peter Yow
Australia
ﾍﾟﾟ0ﾟﾟ

The only limits in life are the ones you allow to exist.

Sia Zapantis
Australia
ﾍﾟﾟ0ﾟﾟ

⠶Finally...

An effective culture of innovation needs to be managed by competent people.

It is the structured process of skills development that allows your leaders and teams to champion innovation.

Greg Kinnaird

Manager and Author
(Organisational Development / Learning and Development / Talent Management)

www.ingramcontent.com/pod-product-compliance
Lightning Source LLC
Chambersburg PA
CBHW021043210326
41598CB00016B/1096